Thomas Edwin Holtham

On Yarra Banks

Lyric chimes and other poems

Thomas Edwin Holtham

On Yarra Banks
Lyric chimes and other poems

ISBN/EAN: 9783744779982

Printed in Europe, USA, Canada, Australia, Japan

Cover: Foto ©Thomas Meinert / pixelio.de

More available books at **www.hansebooks.com**

And other Poems

BY

THOMAS EDWIN HOLTHAM

AUTHOR OF "SOCIETY," "BUDS AND BLOSSOMS," ETC.

MEMBER OF THE AUSTRALIAN INSTITUTE OF JOURNALISTS AND OF THE VICTORIAN REPORTERS' ASSOCIATION.

COPYRIGHT RESERVED.

MELBOURNE:

McCarron, Bird and Co., 479 Collins Street.

1894.

Dedicated

by Permission to

His Excellency the Right Honourable

The Earl of Hopetoun, G.C.M.G.

Governor and Commander-in-Chief

of the

Colony of Victoria.

CONTENTS.

ON YARRA BANKS.

Sunset—Night—Midnight—The Heavens—A Vision---
Break of Day.

NO star was in the heav'ns: a gentle blue
Spread o'er its vast empire, with a bright hue
That lingered in the west, where Phœbus cast
His dying embers, as he slowly passed
On to the other world, whose magic zone
Defines for us the realm that is our own.
The clouds in fragments burst ; onward they fled
With the wild winds that frolicked overhead ;
In charmed confusion, steadily they flew
In bold relief against th' ethereal blue.
At ev'ry step I gazed in serious mood,
Stopped oft to think, grew restless where I stood ;
No thought of fear prevailed, nor did I feel
One weary moment o'er my senses steal.
At last the leaden veil of night was dropt
Over the city wide and tow'rs aloft ;
The skies grew darker even than the earth,
And darker there where first the morn had birth.
Methought a storm was brooding : as I threw
A glance around no tumult met my view,
But a thick darkness, which I could not pierce,
Silent and dead, so melancholy fierce.

B

Then one by one, above, around, below,
The lights gleamed forth, and still they seemed to grow;
Scattered to cause confusion to the sight
And show the darkness of perfected night.
Up in the heavens, up—we know not where,
Deceptive distances defined as air—
All seemed, in silv'ry glow and lambent flame,
Night's glorious transformation to proclaim.
From sullen chimney-tops Vesuvian blaze
Shot distances aloft, and in the daze
Gold-gleaming particles danced madly round,
Like fire-flies tossed 'vhilst winging for the ground.
And deep vibrating notes rose in the air
Of steam-propelled machines ; and ev'rywhere
Late toiling man, who's tempered so to please,
Bespoke his presence by such signs as these.
Shrill whistles blew, the roll of traffic swelled,
And crank and crane their laboured groans impelled ;
Great hammers fell, and clinking sounds went forth,
Titanic art was moulding things of worth.
The modern Babel's truants onward sped
In all directions, scattered and unled ;
Great masses hied along—one could not trace
The lineaments of individual face ;
But the lone heart responsive beat to see
Those swollen streams of freed humanity.
You heard their buzz and hum, betimes the voice
Of some capricious wight who would rejoice ;
Till all at once, with husky, tortured throat,
The barrowmen their presence would denote.

I crossed the bridge : the city loomed immense—
'Twas as if gazing up some eminence ;
The streets ascending narrowed with their lights,
Turrets and floors spun giddy in their flights ;
From point to point reflected brightness shone
Casement and door and crystal orbs upon,
Glinting the cords metallic placed mid-air,
As telling of the subtle currents there ;
While on the walls, in spaces up above,

Fantastic lights and shadows seemed to move;
And as remotely longer still one gazed,
The view enchanted, but the distance dazed.

   I turned me back ; upon that bridge once more
I took my stand and pondered as before ;
The sullen Yarra, darkly in its flow,
Mirrored the stars and meaner lights below.
Upon its bosom lengthening shadows spread,
No ripple ran save where a ray was shed.
Deep, dark recesses lay on either side,
Dark as the caves concealed beneath its tide.
But in the gloom, still darker in repose,
Great masts and bulwarks from the water rose
Defiantly, while tethered now to home—
Those palace-citadels from o'er the foam.
No sound comes from them ; nothing there is heard ;
The seamen sleep, the watchmen have not stirred ;
There is no swing, no frolic with the wind,
Nature and man in purpose have combined.

   Now goes that bell ; how sharp the ring has rolled—
Eight is the strike, the midnight hour is tolled !
It goes upon the air, with no refrain
Save echo's answer eight times back again.
What solitude, what wilderness of night ;
What phantoms float wherever there is light ;
Life's gaysome energy its last has shed,
For all is voiceless, soulless as if dead.
Vain thought ! This hour great heav'n her vigil keeps
Inviolate, while a mighty city sleeps !

   Lo, in Orion's realm those guardian lights
That vaunt the brilliancy of Austral nights ;
Sirius, charmed centre of some universe
Greater than ours, where brighter beams disperse,
But now diminished to a glitt'ring gem
Like other worlds, yet queen o'er all of them.
What glorious galaxies together flash,
Merged in each other, seeming now to clash ;

Or placed alone, but wreathed in endless fold
Of coruscation 'wild'ring to behold.
Centaur and Argo: where, oh, where shall I
Cease marking splendours in this southern sky ?
Mine optics pain ; aha ! my ravished soul,
All heav'n itself is spangling round the Pole !

Still in yon mighty concave spread above,
One token's there of persuasive love,
Which moves our finer faculties and draws
Our adoration and our mute applause.
For, lo, the Cross ! set in its sapphire sea,
Beautifully chaste in that immensity ;
First in procession of those worlds combined,
First in our quest, and ever in our mind ;
That makes her sky the theme of love and song,
The poet's passion as he ponders long ;
The stranger's hope, impatient for the sight
In his approach beneath Australian night.
The dauntless mariner across the Line,
Feels new devotion gazing on that sign ;
And sees in it the covenant of Peace,
Though winds may rage, and ocean's wrath increase.
Watch how he takes his reckonings, and shows
The hour of night from where the jewel glows ;
Ask him the spot, he looks at you in doubt ;
" The Southern Cross ? You cannot point it out ?
There is but one ; you're joking ? Frankly no ;
Up there—straight where my finger's pointing to."

Oh, glorious night ! What brought me forth this hour ?
My pleasure's pain, my pain's another's pow'r ;
My soul lifts up, half mystic to survey
Those clust'ring orbs beside the Milky Way ;
My heart expands in palpitation warm,
My thoughts relax of all terrestrial harm ;
The life I feel is not of common day,
This mould, I know, is not all earthy clay ;
I am not man with those who fear to die,
Or see no future in that lovely sky.

And yet I long still something more to know,
As weak unguided mortal lost below;
Yea, lost on earth, and toiling but to please,
A hostage from so many centuries.
Hope but administers to me that balm
Without which life must lose its ev'ry charm;
Though 'tis opposed to what experience shows—
That pain is *pain*, and pleasure but its throes.

The Yarra winds along, silent and dull;
A lethean stream within the midnight lull;
High up the banks and farther on to trace,
Where circumstance and fancy blend apace,
All seem deserted, motionless, and drear,
As if the doom of judgment entered here.
Hush! there's a voice; I heard it falter then;
I hear it now; I see a throng of men;
Rude, sable folk, to bounding freedom born,
To garment not to ornament forsworn.
Watch how they run and shoot their darts above,
Or dash into that eucalyptus grove;
Climb the stout gum or stately poplar there,
Survey the land unhusbanded but fair;
Wait for their prey and coo-e-e to pursue,
While on some slope appears the kangaroo.
Observe those men who angle by the stream,
Or float on hollowed trunks that know no seam;
Those damsels decked with wattle blooms and flow'rs,
Buoyant with love, or hopeful in all hours;
Those children nude who gambol through the day,
Chase painted insects whizzing by their way;
Or vainly try, with clamour that appals,
To seize the rainbow formed above the Falls.
And, hark! the birds now bursting forth with song,
Flit o'er the twigs that with them sway along;
Their diapason cheers the country round,
And man feels blest when such a spot he's found.

Ha! What is this? Begone my dream, begone!
Methought this hour that I had gazed upon
The wild mysterious Past, and learned to know

How things existed centuries long ago.
There's nought to view that ancient art can claim,
There's nought to call but by its common name,
Now that the eastern portals glow with fire,
And flashing lights to highest heav'n aspire.
Lo, revelations grow on ev'ry side,
Progress advance with Liberty allied;
Beauty and blessedness, while all are gay,
And Melbourne revels in her golden day.

·····

WESTMINSTER ABBEY.

Written after a visit in September, 1875.

MY heart was sore disturbed, my courage shook,
As from this world a sudden plunge I took
Amid a thousand years.   I stared aghast,
Because I breathed the influence of the Past,
And felt a new creation o'er me steal
That chafened not on Time's progressive wheel.
My temples ached, my pulse the faster played :
It was a world that grew not nor decayed :—
It was the Past ; the mute, mysterious ken
That purifies the reasonings of men.
The Present was forgot : it seemed as fled
To regions of the unforgotten dead ;
Care had resigned its seat within my breast,
And passions human all were hushed to rest.
What silence reigned around! the pure, the deep,
Alike the spell of those who, dying, sleep,
Forgetful of their ills ; while Love keeps watch
With voice subdued the sparks of life to catch.

The world without to heedlessness consigned,
Was lost to sight ; I felt not of its kind ;
And speechless stood the while, immured, alone,
As influenced by the animated stone
As of estate akin.   What feeling this ?
Around prevailed the dignity, the bliss,
The awe, esteem, the sympathetic gloom
For those who've passed the universal doom
And upward flown to heav'n ; leaving on earth
A people proud to estimate their worth.

I passed me slowly on and stood again ;
Enough had been in ev'ry moment then
To mollify the trammel and the strife,
The seething ills, the dissonance of life.
With lighter spirits flown to nether spheres,
My bosom heaved with what it most endears,
What man must e'er adore.   'Twas joy sublime,
The pure, unruffled, welcome at all time;
That elevates the soul with humbler pride,
To know in form we're such as those who've died—
Those of the mighty dead.   'Twas joy that spoke
The future when this mortal dream has broke ;
And makes the fears of death that men degrade
For once depart and seek th' infernal shade.
We hate the sunshine, we prefer the gloom ;
We love the trust, the chillness of the tomb.

What Pantheon this with lofty grey-grown aisles,
That with its walls of manifold designs,
Erects itself on earth and stands alone
In rivalry to Egypt, Greece and Rome ?
What marble there that teems with life again ?
Methinks it moves from where the bones have lain.
What spot is this, the slab that I survey ?
Methought a form ascending passed away.
What voice is that, as rising from the bier ?
Methinks 'tis one, who living, lives not here.

Is this the Past ?   How glorious then to die,
To leave the world behind and upward fly

Away from earth's existence, which we hate,
And 'mong the seraph stars to meditate:
To cast asunder what we grieve to know,
For life is false, a counterfeit below.
Is this the Past? How pleasant then to die;
Through yonder space, beyond the sun to fly;
To never cease till angels bright we meet
And all the stars are glitt'ring at our feet:
To mount into the future and behold
Ourselves immortals in the realms of gold.
Hush! Tell me not to what the flesh is heir,
For ills have I, the chains of life I bear;
And in my breast the work is being done,
And ev'ry day a link is snapped and gone.

Is that the Future? Thus to die and be
From slander, pain, from sin and sorrow free;
To breathe empyrean airs and yet be known
Through long eternity from zone to zone?
The thought be holy now, for where I tread
Repose in golden peace th' illustrious dead;
The very soil is flesh to dust returned—
To ashes human: flesh that once had burned
With all the pow'r, the talent of our kind,
And filled with joy the universal mind.

Untired my wistful gaze, on ev'ry side
Death I behold in one has all allied;
Those of the ages long since passed away,
Those from our midst who left but yesterday;
All in the magic circle of our view,
The king, the subject, and the rivals too.
The warrior here, at peace with all the world,
Has sheathed his sword; his flag for e'er is furled;
The trumpet falls no more upon his ear,
Nor battle's din, nor vict'ry's ringing cheer.
The orator is mute: the day has passed
When, like the reed that trembles in the blast,
The country heard his voice and sought to find
Its aspirations in his giant mind.

So too his ablest foe. The hoary sage,
Whose meditative eye had scanned the age,
Who in the majesty of thought explored
The heav'ns, the earth, each intellectual hoard—
Has ceased from labours dear to memory,
Reposing now within this sanctuary.
Oh, where is he who born to lays sublime,
Concealed so oft the onward flight of time
By bursts melodious from the golden lyre—
The gentle poet with Promethean fire?
Methinks I hear the echo of his song
The cloisters, niches and the tombs among;
'Tis here he lies, within this sacred ground;
How song indeed has hallowed all around!

Hence thought debased, corruption's awful taint!
Let life be bliss without the woful feint;
Hence what is mortal, what is flesh decay,
And soar my soul to distant worlds away!
Diminish earth—thou whom by Sol revealed
Of sloth, of sin and shame, of scars unhealed;
Evanish then thou one dark spot of night
Amid the flood of universal light—
Thou who art doomed to burst thy bonds asunder,
And with a crash, a dreadful roll of thunder,
Hurled to be then with one tumultuous groan,
To pits unfathomed and to depths unknown!

The sun was sinking fast: the feeble light
That spread within was hurrying into night;
Chill winds arose and gliding gently by
Seemed to intone the day's departing sigh.
From nave to choir, from clustered columns tall,
Protracted shadows solemnly did fall
And rest upon the tombs, as like the pall
That screens the dead and speaks of death to all.
I heard the footsteps gently fade away
Of those who pondered there; nor did I stay,
But, as with heart from bliss for ever hurled,
I left the Past and sought the living world.

INDIA.

WHEN order first confusion hurled and from
    Cimmerian night
    There sprung unnumbered silver orbs with
    universal light:
When Earth no more the pathless space inanimate,
    impure,
Rolled headlong, but with measured pace the ages to
    endure—
'Twas then when Nature's hand was raised, and gazing
    from her throne,
She cast around her bounties and divided zone from zone—
That India, favoured country, in her destiny assigned,
With a sunny lap of pleasure and an ostentatious mind,
Bore away in exultation choicest treasures: and her land
Seemed luxuriant with the foliage by spicy breezes fanned
Brighter skies above her spreading, north and south and
    east and west,
Iris tints now intertwining with the blue ethereal blest,
Spoke of Nature in her grandest where the souls
    immortal trod,
And the eye of man was tempted to the dwelling of his
    God.
Golden morn and purple sunset o'er her heav'n their
    charms revealing,
Fall of twilight, flash Promethean and the mighty
    thunder pealing—
All of these in their sublimest, with foreboding clouds of
    rain,
That at mid-year rise in phalanx from the foaming,
    wrathful main—
Speak of Him who in His judgment from the golden
    throne on high
Shaped the world and gave it being as a jewel in the sky;
Gave to India such of treasures as would dazzle all the
    rest;
And in prophecy is Japheth of the tents of Shem possessed.

Monarch of this wondrous system, thou magician of
    the spheres,
Lo, around thee in thy splendour spinning out the
    thousand years,
Orbs that glancing thy effulgence down remotest walks
    of time,
Swell the harmony of Nature and the order is sublime.
But see in thy dominion from the Orient to the west
Life's pulsations in their action rouse the living from
    their rest,
What time the dusky mountain tops the skies descendent
    span,
Catch first the herald beams of morn that over Hindostan
Brighter grow and still the brighter, till the fast-
    approaching night
Drops its mantle over Nature and the world is lost to
    sight.
But the day from early coming, ever varying in its hue,
Lives at noontide in the grandeur of loved cerulean blue;
And the eye of man is dazzled as he glances everywhere,
And his heart fills with devotion as he humbly breathes
    a pray'r.
From yonder ancient temple—ruins now that long have
    lain
On the Deccan Ghauts, o'erlooking the far-receding vale,
Have I gazed betimes in silence, it was silence that was
    awe,
And methought the scene for certain in a vision then I
    saw,
For the charm it was continuous and it held me in the
    plight
Of him peeping into fairyland at fairy hours of night.
There perhaps in yonder temple, in seclusion all alone,
Kneeled the poor misguided jogi praying to his god of
    stone ;
There, perhaps, the little maiden decked with wreaths of
    marigold,
And with jewels rare and costly all her little failings told ;
Looking like the gentle lambkin, hardly knowing what
    was sin,

And yet pleading for forgiveness with a contrite heart
within.
The childless matron surely there repaired with lamen-
tation,
From the censure of her people, their heartless condem-
nation ;
Wringing hands before Bhavani in her superstitious
dread ;
Kneeling there without her jewels, kneeling with uncovered
head ;
Saying rather than a curse be in the eyes of all the world,
May the wrath of mighty Siva be the moment at her
hurled.

How have passed the days primeval when a people
proud and blest
Left the world to its own kindred, interposing not the rest ;
Satisfied that their dominion, great and stocked with
wealth unending,
Needed not exotic genius nor the alien befriending.
With their own and native talent in the plethory of pride,
Fought they through the gloom surrounding, one and all
in one allied ;
Filled with hope and with ambition—it was zeal for what
was wanting,
For the reach of all that grandeur which their fancy was
so haunting.
Plodded they for years together in the craft of their
direction,
Till their genius soared its highest and their work was
called Perfection ;
Then, alas !—oh, hateful mortal, what are we but self-
adorers !
What is life but fitful longing and a service of misnomers !
They, enchanted of their powers, gazed with quickening
emotion,
Till in spell they were o'erpowered, and their love
became devotion.
Thus it was they were corrupted, there's the idol ; there
it stands ;

Staggered they by native genius, worshipping the work
  of hands ;
Smitten down by superstition, triumphed o'er by indolence,
While the gloom that once had vanished now was
  gathering as dense.
Then they formed the dreadful Yama, or the Lakhshmi
  of their dreams,
As the moment brought its horror with the joy that
  intervenes ;
Then their pantheon was swarming with the gods of
  their creation,
Shapes fantastic, host infernal, yielding nought but sure
  damnation.

  Here the scene is changed for ever. Not in Ind again
    there gathers
All that's noblest in the mortal and the glory of her
  fathers ;
Hosts have come and been ejected, conq'ring legions have
  assembled,
Thousand times the fate of Empire in the balance now
  has trembled.
But to one above all other, to the foremost of her kind,
'Neath whose flag the meanest mortal scans the empire
  of the mind ;
'Neath whose sway the fretted bondsman feels no more
  the cumbrous chain,
But divides the rule of kindred upon the world's domain—
Is the task decreed by Heav'n to restore the ancient
  glory
That is lost, for ages crumbled, and but pining now in
  story.

  Who has roamed the pathless jungle at the early hour
    of morn,
As the orphan gleams of sunshine, with the wanton
  breezes borne,
Shot amongst and through the branches, while the birds
  that slept the night,
Flapped their wings and tossed their feathers, leaping,
  singing with delight ?

Lo, the herd of wild creation with their roars of brazen
    thunder,
As the hurried bounds of echo seem to root the woods
    asunder,
Panting past from den to streamlet in the vagaries of hue,
Lording now o'er one another and submitting to the few.
Times have been when in the border of the region have
    I strayed,
On the carpet laid about me of the dead leaves in the
    glade;
And I peered into the darkness that receding darkened
    more,
Till there seemed the blank eternal of the future that's
    before;
And I feared to loiter further where no trace of man had
    been,
For holy that alone is which no human eye has seen.
'Neath the father of the forest from whose bearded trunks
    descending,
Thousand limbs that grasp each other, stout and strong
    and interblending,
Have I gazed as from the nave of some ancient pile ornate,
With the columns straight above me, and my bosom was
    elate.
There around the arches clustered in the luxury of choice,
There the niches were unnumbered; and I heard the
    bulbul's voice,
From its choral seat above me of the sylvan fane rejoice.
Busy sounds come from the jungle; all that's life is
    joyous there;
Where the blossoms spread their fragrance, where the
    fruits are rich and rare;
Where the pathways lead a little and diminish unaware.

  See you yonder cosy village 'mid the fields of rice and
    corn,
Smiling on the painted country in the healthy rays of
    morn;
Through the day its toilsome moments speed a merry
    flight along,
As the water-wheel is grating and the ryot sings a song.

There beneath the thatch and bamboo, chiming in a
    roundelay,
Sit two gentle-minded consorts at the handmill half the day;
While the children nude and noisy gather near the sacred
    cow,
And the skulking dog is watching the green parrots on
    the bough.
There beside the shady *babul* nymphs and naiads morn
    and even,
With their many-coloured garments in the mellowness of
    heaven,
Gather round with merry laughter, treading with a fairy
    tread
At the well of their forefathers, the memento of the dead.
There the gossip knows its highest with the foe and
    friend and neighbour,
There are witnessed hate and passion and the half of
    household labour;
'Mid the clang of copper vessels and the bangles and the
    charms,
And the dripping of well water, and those innocent alarms,
Changeless through the world inconstant, its amities and
    strife,
Are the modest Hindu maiden and the faithful Hindu wife.
    Cradle of a thousand races, Ind with varied beauties
      vying,
Happier fate is now approaching, better seasons now
    are nighing;
More to purpose are thy genius and philosophy applied,
Man and man are now but brothers and their rights are
    not denied.
Lo, the Himalayan ranges, nearest spot to holy heaven,
Where the bleak and azure concave by the flash and
    thunder riven,
Rise majestic o'er thy empire and with grandeurs yet
    untold
Swell the awful voice of Nature, that deepening is rolled
Down the dark and miry hollows, down the lone ravines
    resounding,
Through the chill and soulless caverns and from crag to
    crag rebounding:

But the tongue of man is feeble, and vain, how very vain,
In his littleness he pictures the dignified domain.
Lo, the graceful maiden Gunga, river goddess, o'er the
waters
Bear the emblematic lily—she the fairest of all daughters,
From whose bounty pour abundance and the smiling,
fruitful land
Feels the influence of the donor and the cultivator's hand;
And the crowds assemble round her with brimming
hearts and eyes,
And watch her trailing garment as it sparkles 'neath the
skies.
Say, O Ind, with all thy treasures framed and costly and
unending,
Say, with all thy grand allurements and their varied
blessings rending,
If thy place is not exalted, and in thee there's not to find
What is noblest in creation, loveliest to the human mind?
Chaster art than thine is nameless, art that lives with
thee alone,
Art that forms the mountain palace, gives vitality to
stone;
All that sweet and charmed profusion, the intricacies of
thought,
Speak the zeal of thy devotion from the fanes on which
they're wrought:
And the wares of thine own making now have roused to
worthy praise
Nations once that knew thee only as the germ of other days.

It is morn, the sunbeams brighten, but the noon has
scarce begun:
Reformation, move thou onward, for the day is not yet
done;
And the task is left unfinished, thousands yet in woe are
plunged,
Superstition must be conquered, what is dross must be
expunged:
Thousand changes still are needed; Britain, raise on
high thy wand,
And restore the ancient glory of the once ennobled land.

LYRIC CHIMES.

DARLING GRACE.

AS thy beauty's beaming now,
　　　　　Darling Grace,
Let me pay to thee my vow,
　　　　　Darling Grace;
If the task you will allow,
　　　　　I can trace
In thine eyes a glow of pleasure,
In thine heart a precious treasure,
Love unsullied without measure,
　　　　　Darling Grace.

Days seem ages without thee,
　　　　　Darling Grace;
Dreadful moments pass by me,
　　　　　Darling Grace,
If perchance I fail to see
　　　　　Thy sweet face.
And in my bosom dwells a storm,
My heart dejected sleeps forlorn;
'Tis awful from thee to be torn,
　　　　　Darling Grace.

Listen to this hapless youth,
　　　　　Darling Grace;
He will die for thee, forsooth,
　　　　　Darling Grace,
For to tell thee an untruth
　　　　　'Twould be base.
Pure thought and virtue now I see,
A heart too gentle dwells in thee;
Say only *yes*, and I am free,
　　　　　Darling Grace.

c

THE WAYS OF THE WORLD.

IT is so with the whole of the world,
  Contentment here never does dwell:
We must live in its pleasures, then shortly be hurled.
Or must fly so soon as its truths we've unfurled :—
  Alas! 'tis a miniature hell.

Here deception is practised by all ;
  Oh ! what would I give to be free:
We must go as sly fortune invites us to call,
And then rapidly rise, and then rapidly fall
  Into depths where we shudder to be.

Goodly words are a pleasure unknown,
  They come when we care for them not :
E'en the monarch who sits on the stateliest throne,
Has a heart that's already with misery outgrown:
  The greatest must wither and rot.

Friends are many when harvest is ripe,
  They fall off as harvest decays :
Oh, man! art thou born of so worthless a type,
And never canst thou all thy evils outwipe ?
  What will be the end of thy days!

Everything has beginning and end ;
  A time is allotted to all :
And the greatest must even on something depend,
Th' Almighty sole power does ne'er to *one* send ;
  Sometimes we must go to the wall.

The old sire was once a young boy,
  The mistress was once a sweet maid ;
But Time stole upon them and dissolved each joy,
Old Age did their spirits and beauty destroy,
  And leaves them to mourn in the shade.

E'en the earth, which is so full of pleasure,
  Some day from its bonds must be torn :
Alas! it must lose ev'ry grain of its treasure,
Its pomp, its dominion, its joys without measure:
  The world has a future to mourn !

MY OWN, MY SWEET BRUNETTE.

THOUGH torn away from thy dear side,
　Though borne upon the sea,
No other thoughts in me abide,
　For love I think of thee.
Thy phantom flies before me, dear ;
　Ah, how could I forget
When breezes whisper in my ear—
　" Thine own, thy sweet brunette ? "

Scorn not the love, break not the chain
　That sacred is to me ;
Though fast I fly across the main
　I must return to thee.
Think of the heart that loved thee long,
　The heart that loves thee yet ;
Turn not thy face, but hear my song,
　My own, my sweet brunette.

Ah ! whither must I comfort find
　When I am far away ?
Still shall thy face live in my mind,
　And be my life each day.
Yes, yes, thy face shall be my light,
　As when at first we met ;
In visions shall our hearts unite,
　My own, my sweet brunette.

Though lands may screen me from thy view,
　And gulfs set us apart,
They cannot turn my love from you,
　Nor change this faithful heart.
The vessel further sails along,
　Each move do I regret :
Adieu, my love; Oh, hear my song—
　My own, my sweet brunette.

MISFORTUNE.

OH, how could I another day
    Upon this luckless region stay?
Alas! my woes will not away,
        Nor e'en an hour abide.

Each day I find is darker still,
My dreams of joy I can't fulfil,
Misfortune seeks me at her will,
        And pains my breathless side.

I feel my heart is weaker now,
A fever teems upon my brow,
An ague shakes me too I vow,
        And clasps me to the breast.

And who could stay amid such woe,
Where all is shade with not a glow?
Will not kind Heav'n spare here below
        A spot where I might rest?

It seems to me the more I try
To raise myself and ope mine eye,
A whisper comes "Thou sinner, die!
        Thy ling'ring's o'er on earth."

I cannot live as others do,
I cannot seek a prospect new,
I dare not laugh nor smile as you;
        Joy left me at my birth.

Where'er I go no words of joy
Pour forth my troubles to destroy;
I'm now misfortune's darling boy—
        So 'tis proclaimed by all.

No star will shine upon my head,
I know not if I've been misled,
But I must lie upon my bed,
    And there await my call.

Some speak to me of foreign shores,
Where I might hope for friendly doors;
How can I stir ? Each gale that roars
    A thousand ills infest.

Forsaken here, where shall I roam ?
What spot can I pronounce my home ?
Not till my spirit sad has flown
    To seek eternal rest.

SONNET: FRUITS AND FLOWERS.

FRUITS and Flowers! What blisses they contain
  To charm the eye and soothe the sighing breast;
The heart leaps forth and bursts its ev'ry chain,
  While fancy dawns with visions truly blest.
  Nature unlocks her wealth ; her grassy vest
Glows with Aurora's dews on ev'ry plain ;
The syren warblers tune the choir again,
  And trees are in their sheeny verdure drest.
View how the golden orbs, dependent, swing ;
  Lo, how the varied gems caress the showers ;
I would this life were one unceasing Spring,
  And made, of course, of only fruits and flowers.
Then would unclouded joys enwrap the world,
And woes be to Cimmerian darkness hurled.

CENTENNIAL EXHIBITION DAY.

Melbourne, 1st August, 1888.

I.

RING out the bells of joy and peace, the gladsome
    news peal forth,
  From Pole to Pole the song of Peace convey ;
To the people and the thrones of the east and west and
    north
  The Southern World bids welcome on this day.
A hundred years have fleeted by, and yon unerring sun
  Shall mark the advent of a brighter age,
When sons shall scan the golden scroll of what their
    sires had done,
  And seek enrolment on th' unwritten page.
What saith the Genius of this soil ?   What record shall
    she bear
  Of deeds of triumph falsifying fate ?
Wrought by the early pilgrims who achieved what giants
    dare,
  And gave us the sovereignty of State.

THE GENIUS OF AUSTRALIA.

Honour eternal be their share, and undiminished fame ;
What rarer gift can earth bestow than what their labours
    claim ?
Men who have toiled for men to come, unthought in
    human ken,
From out the multitude we say, these, verily, are MEN.

II.

Behold the transformation now ; what glorious light
    defines
  The present from the past ; and as ye gaze,
The darksome forest now recedes, and manly art combines
  The bright and newer continent to raise.
The dismal swamp and arid waste have fled and given
    place
  To Ceres and Pomona in their bloom ;

And while all Nature gaily smiles, in triumph comes apace
  Flora bedecked with garlands of perfume.
Grandeur and grace on every side, surpassing fairy dreams,
  And Industry with all her useful train,
Joins hand with Commerce; while we hear in all our
  wondrous schemes,
  " Advance Australia !" ever in refrain.

THE GENIUS OF AUSTRALIA.

What's sweeter to a nation's pride than genius that
  commands
The praise and admiration of the men of other lands?
And at this day a hundred years 'mong nations young
  in age,
Ye've seized the spirit of the times your future to presage.

III.

Joyous the day we celebrate, and in our feast and song
  We meet in peace the nations of the world;
And, lo, amidst the trophies raised, and o'er the glitt'ring
  throng,
  The banner of the Southern Cross unfurled.
Melbourne, Queen City of the South, resplendent in the
  dawn,
  Now see her all her magic skill employ,
To greet the vast assembled host on Exhibition morn,
  And hail her people with redoubled joy.
Hark! what is that? The Psalm of Praise; the music
  floats along;
  And hear betimes the diapason swell;
A thousand voices from the choir burst forth in vig'rous
  song,
  That hurtles where the mountain echoes dwell.

THE GENIUS OF AUSTRALIA.

Long shall this day remembered be, on which we see unite
Fair Oceania's people, her beauty, wealth, and might;
The future looms before ye now, 'tis shimmering and
  bright,
And at the threshold as ye stand let th' historic muse
  indite.

GWENDA.

I KNEW not Love when first I heard its name,
    Methought the rich could but its treasure claim;
Some precious gem, some smoothly polished stone,
Such I believed was Love, and seldom known.
Of Love I often heard, but never learnt,
Heard people speak how Love their hearts had burnt:
'Twas then I thought it fire from heav'n above,
Some scorching orb; yea, such I thought was Love.

My mind was ripened more, and then I thought
Love was a thing of chance which mankind sought:
Bestowed by Heav'n on man, or perhaps, hell,
But which of two I'm sure I could not tell.
Thinking, believing, thoughts together came;
'Twas now a gem or jewel, then a flame;
In these perplexities my heart would move,
Caused by the ardent wish to know of Love.

But since, O Gwenda, since your peerless face
Brought to my view charms which no other grace,
I've lived as one enchanted; and thy glance
Has held me bound whilst pleading for a chance.
Those locks, that bosom's pure ethereal calm,
Roused in me rapture with attendant charm;
Wisdom innate, that with my conscience strove,
Half said it was, half said it was not, Love.

Quick to the flowery vale then did I rush,
Telling my tale unconscious of the flush;
Telling the hermit there within the grove;
" Yes," he exclaimed, " why, that is nought but love."
And now, most prized of all, here will I lay
My heart for thine, and wilt thou tell me nay?
Oh, scorn me not, and may in heav'n above
Be sealed the union of our mutual love.

THE DISOWNED.

BITTER he said was life; and as he spake
   I with emotion saw his bosom quake;
Bitter he said was life; he spoke too true;
His visage seemed of ghostly, palish hue.
As if before a phantom there I stood,
Fixed to the spot and chilly ran my blood.
I did not fear, nor did I feel within
The pressing weakness through my limbs begin;
I only wondered, could not understand
How he all bone could move a nerveless hand;
And puzzled he should speak, myself so scan,
That living skeleton of lifeless man.

Bitter he said was life; and in each word
A hollow sound a feeble thrill I heard;
Often he paused and gasped as if for breath,
He a *sure* victim of *uncertain* death.
Oh! 'twas a painful thing to see his form,
In him at once the haggard, pale, forlorn;
Hapless and poor; homeless and left to live
On the rare charities the world might give;
His ev'ry beat of heart too truly gave
A nearer pathway to the gaping grave.

Bare were his feet and gashed by many a stone,
And ev'ry gash but seemed a parted bone:
His tattered garments—rags that hung profuse—
Were rotting quite through age and constant use.
A rimless hat he wore, cut, soiled, and crushed,
His locks of varied length hung thick with dust;
And in his hand a shapeless stick he bore,
With which he trudged and passed the city o'er.

Bitter he said was life. " And *why*?" said I;
" Is there not o'er thee spread a pitying sky?
There is a God; He watches thee from there;
'Twas He who made thee and for thee will care.
He will look down though now thy life be dim,
And in the future take thee unto Him.

Despair not, youth ; surrender to thy lot ;
'Tis but a shade that keeps no certain spot ;
'Twill pass and leave thee brighter than at first,
Not in a land as this, an earth so curst,
But in a realm where seraphs only dwell,
Whose countless beauties man could never tell."
He listened with a quivering lip and eye,
Not knowing when or how to make reply ;
His looks were vacant, but I could surmise
They besought my charity and not advice.
Taking the trifle I could barely spare,
He thanked me, blessed me with a vacant stare ;
Then onward went, alas ! a spectre grim,
Skeleton ghost, most miserably thin.
Nor could I cease my gaze till he had passed
Athwart my view.   And still that form aghast
My vision haunts with unalarming fear ;
At morn, at night methinks I see it here.
Each shadow cast I dream 'tis his alone,
Whom now the world seems quite ashamed to own ;
He who through hapless lot and days of gloom
Appears no man of earth but of the tomb.

———··►X◄··———

SONNET: TO A DOG.

OH, gen'rous friend of man, whose loving heart
     Grows brighter at each act of kindness shown ;
    Thy love is pure and ardent, 'tis thine own ;
No mortal shares of it the weakest part.
Thy comp'ny's constant ; office, home, or mart,
    Thou'lt follow on to leave me not alone :
    Contentment fills thee with the meanest bone.
At dang'rous night the first alarm to start.
To show thy gratitude thou wag'st thy tail,
    And lick'st my hand with bark sincere ;
    My best of friends, in troubles thou art near ;
Thy love for me dost o'er thyself prevail.
Then I could not thy face from me withdraw ;
Come, faithful friend, give me your darling paw.

OH, THINK ME NOT LONELY.

OH, think me not lonely because I'm alone,
   And have nothing aloud to relate;
There's enough to employ each moment our own,
   In picturing futurity's state.
Should sorrow encumber the smiles that have been,
   And I move with a pitiful groan,
Oh, think them not real in what they would seem,
   For they are not because I'm alone.

In the silence of thought a world does arise,
   And I mirror each beautiful scene;
Each wavers and sinks like a bird in the skies,
   And I think I've been dreaming a dream.
But should you suspect I have anguish at heart,
   And a tremor that weakens the tone,
Oh, believe not what fancy might to thee impart,
   For they are not because I'm alone.

Ah! vain, very vain are the joys we survey,
   And how shallow the glory of man,
For the breath of a moment can bear him away
   From the scenes where his projects began.
Yet, should you discover a mark on my brow,
   And a furrow there always unknown,
Oh, believe not promptings of fancy; for know
   That they are not because I'm alone.

Oh, think me not lonely because I'm alone,
   And my silence is not my regret;
Have we nought to think of but murmur and moan,
   Live there not fairer prospects as yet?
Should you picture in me each shadow of woe,
   Should you think all my rapture has flown,
Then remember the duties of life here below
   Cannot make me feel I'm alone.

AT A WATERFALL.

In Front of the Planters' Association Hall, Dimbula, Ceylon.

DO not fill this cup but that I breathe
    Thanks unto heav'n for this refreshing draught ;
For this I know, that pangs of lesser death,
    Which do not bring with them the fatal shaft,
Had tortured me three hours on earth beneath,
    Till Nature's richest bev'rage I had quaffed.
Oh, have you ever tasted sudden bliss?
In such a state kiss such a cup as this.

I fill this cup, and as the bubbles rise,
    Richer than Rhenish wine can ever know,
My heart's delight is pictured in mine eyes,
    The sense of languor back from me I throw:
Thus do I feel and hope to realise
    Untasted bliss in the cup's overflow.
Have you not sipped this liquid e'er before ?
Then drink, and you will stretch your hand for more.

This cup is filled with what kind heav'n provides,
    Pure crystal water from the mountain stream,
That never in its downward course abides,
    But gushes forth, bright in the noonday beam ;
And with its melody at night it glides
    The cascade pictured in a fairy dream.
Take this and taste ; by this may it be shown
Health's best preserver—if ye have not known.

These weary hours a stranger here have I
    Lost and retraced my steps without delay;
Meeting with those whose efforts did defy
    Each other's genius to explain the way :
One foot-sore trav'ller still had held me by,
    Bound for his native village on that day.
Hot ? 'Twas indeed.   We saw the steam arise
From out the earth, dazzling each other's eyes.

On, on we went still higher up the mount,
    His language strange, my signs in awkward haste,
The distance done, the distance yet to count,
    Of disappointment only then to taste—
Methought to rest by the first stream or fount
    That from some cliff would hurl her waters waste :
But duty's call forbade a moment's stay,
And hope gave promise of a better day.

How nature revelled there in all her wealth,
    Around the charms of brightest tints beguiled ;
The loveliest flow'rs, some peeping as by stealth
    From out the hedgerows growing densely wild ;
And busy man, seen in the bloom of health,
    On man's estate to toil is reconciled.
Hark, now, that splash, the streamlet dash along,
The blackbird's note, the redbreast's noonday song.

On yonder peaks, from out the sunny boughs,
    Inviting villas gaze upon the scene ;
While the nude herdsman watches o'er his cows,
    His mate a ring-tailed mongrel large and lean :
And on the slopes the sheep demurely browse,
    And crows assert the knaves they've always been.
These pass we on, till faint at last I stay
Where a rustic mansion stops me on my way.

Oh, nobly simple, timber lodge, retreat !
    Wherein thy mountain chiefs for miles that be,
Joyed in the round of every season, meet
    To talk and taste the qualities of tea.
Ha ! thee I've found at last, though sore of feet,
    For three long hours I've been in quest of thee.
Now of this stream that tumbles at thy door,
I'll drink success to thee for evermore.

Within thy hall thy politics are few,
    Here Tea and Commerce hold undoubted sway ;
And social gaieties receive their due,
    And labour sometimes knows its holiday.
And midnight frisking thou has seen, 'tis true,
    But will not gravest men betimes be gay ?
I fill this cup from the torrent at thy door,
And drink success to thee for evermore.

NAN, THE FISHERMAN'S DAUGHTER.

NOT far from Albion's happy shore,
   Where hoary cliffs ascend,
Where swells the deep Atlantic roar,
   Unfailing, without end—

There might ye see amid the rocks,
   That form long ages pile,
A home that raging ocean mocks
   In pleasant fisher style.

'Tis sad to tell the mournful tale
   That rings within my ear,
Whilst far I view the gliding sail
   That line the hemisphere.

Each wave that beats the craggy steep,
   And louder in its moan,
Makes desolation doubly deep
   In that once-pleasant home.

But, hark! the seamew cries afar,
   He flies the wat'ry plain;
He shoots across the rising star
   That lights the distant main.

Alas! the cottage 'mid the rocks
   Deserted lies alone;
The form once with those hoary locks
   From there long, long has flown.

No voice is heard, no youthful shout,
   No taper lights the room,
And fast the door is locked without,
   Whilst silence spreads her gloom.

Ten long, long summers now have passed
   Since that once mournful day,
When th' inmate of that home I last
   Perceived upon my way.

'Twas ere the sun lit up the morn ;
   He rose and thus began—
" Come, with our nets let us begone ;
   What say you, daughter Nan ?"

His daughter, Nan, a lovely maid,
   Obedient to his will,
Arose and to the beach she strayed
   To get the nets their fill.

A little bark was put afloat,
   With fishers brave and strong ;
Nan's father too jumped in the boat
   And joined the sturdy throng.

Each face a pleasant smile possessed
   Their fortunes for to reap ;
Anticipation roused the breast
   To treasures of the deep.

The vessel left its island shore,
   Well trimmed, well manned, and tight ;
And while it stepped the waters o'er,
   Nan waved her 'kerchief white.

She viewed it pass the rocky pier,
   'Twas there she kept her eyes on ;
And soon no more she saw it steer,
   It passed the dim horizon.

The noon had passed ; the orb of day
   Its task had finished nigh ;
And soon from earth it made away,
   Whilst darkness hurried by.

In vain did Nan possess a grace,
   No boat approached the shore ;
Little thought she her sire's face
   On earth she'd see no more.

Fear soon did take her youthful form,
   She saw the billows rise ;
Athwart the pier rose high the storm,
   That dimmed her eager eyes.

And soon the hours one by one
    Betook a rapid flight,
While sad she stood to gaze upon
    The canopy of night.

No form's still seen, no bark appears
    To lash atween the wave :
She cries with lifted eyes in tears—
    " The Lord alone can save."

She turned with sorrow, all forlorn
    She sought her cottage home,
In hopes that ere the break of morn
    Her aged sire would come.

She kept a taper burning bright,
    She sat beside the door,
To give her good old father light
    When he should reach the shore.

She had no mother ; no, for she
    Had died when Nan was young :
And Nan now dreamt of melody,
    The hymns her mother sung.

Slow seemed the hours to onward pace
    For vigil hid their flight ;
No ray the darkness seemed to chase,
    'Twas veritable night.

But, oh ! the joys of bygone days
    Had now for ever fled ;
For scarce had Phœbus spread his rays
    When this to her was said—

" Alas ! sweet Nan; weep not in grief ;
    Thy father will not come ;
He's gone (for joys on earth are brief),
    To seek a better home.

" Last night the storm king rose in rage,
    Which made his kingdom dark ;
And ev'ry wave did battle rage,
    And leap thy father's bark.

"He bravely stood the tempest's shock,
 Which took him by surprise;
His bark now rests upon the rock,
 Whilst 'neath the sea he lies."

The words came from one of the crew,
 The only rescued man:
He turned his steps and bade adieu
 To sorrow-stricken Nan.

She heard the news with many tears,
 And left that very day;
But where she's gone (tho' ten long years
 Have passed) I cannot say.

And still upon that rocky shore
 Her home is seen to stand,
Braving the wild Atlantic roar
 That rings the rugged strand.

Tho' voice of music is not heard
 Within that silent home,
Ye far away might hear the bird
 That skips the ocean foam.

And by its shade the fishers pass,
 Who never once do fail
To tell the folk who kindly ask
 Of them the mournful tale.

————————⚔————————

AT GALLE FACE, COLOMBO.

REMOTE in the offing where Sol is descending
 The ocean comes up in full grandeur and state;
  And at the day's ending,
  In rich colours blending,
The chariot wheels gather the foam they create.
  Now rolling and rising,
  All objects despising,
See the billows advance at a more rapid rate;

D

They swell with a motion
That tells of commotion,
Then suddenly halting, they seem to abate.
But ascending once more,
With a charge and a roar,
They come as before, but in force twice as great;
But on reaching the shore,
They but scatter it o'er
With ripples that beat a retreat precipitate.
And so on, thus daily
This play goes on gaily,
While the sun, moon, and stars in their orbits rotate.

In ev'ry direction, where'er the eye's turning,
Tall palms shoot at random, a shelter to spread;
Kind nature's discerning
The thanksgiving earning
Of the trav'ller who feels the cool shade o'er his head.
See them stoop as a warden
O'er housetop and garden,
And lean on each other or aught else instead.
See them o'er the lake dangle,
Wherein the stars spangle,
And gaze down below at the fish in their bed.
Now with the wind dancing,
And moving and prancing,
Yet housing the birds from the gale that have fled—
In all our distressing
They prove a true blessing,
By giving to man both his drink and his bread:
And in any condition
They make us provision,
And furnish in common the cottager's shed.

Aye, this is a picture on which long could I gaze,
'Tis with all that is lovely and cheering replete;
Where little folks rattle
With innocent prattle,
And improve the first lesson—the use of the feet.

Where with look that perplexes
The opposite sexes,
A friend, foe or stranger right face to face meet;
Where decked out in fashion,
And full of love's passion,
Both young men and maidens so studiedly greet;
Who in their opinion
Hold perfect dominion,
And their elders in wisdom and etiquette beat.
Here too will there gather
Both grandam and father,
To take exercise—for the salt air's a treat.
While gossiping woman,
With feelings inhuman,
Struts for scandal to publish next day in the street.

Here Lunka displays ev'ry race of her soil,
The wealthy, the beggared, the highborn, the low;
As for those who turmoil,
Or as sojourners toil,
You count them by scores as men pass to and fro.
Oh, the picture's quite to my notion,
I love all this life and commotion,
The strange voices of people who come up and go
The clatter of hoofs and the chime
Of the cow-bells that ring out of time,
And the sweet sounds of music that's distant and slow.
Let me look as of yore with devotion
On the broad expanse of the ocean,
And the works of the one Omnipotent know.
Let me stroll on the beach
And inquiringly reach
The shells and the shingles the tidal waves throw;
Admitting that truly in vain
Men boast of the knowledge they gain,
When the lesser things 'round them embarrass them so.

ON SEEING AN ILLEGIBLE INSCRIPTION ON A TOMBSTONE.

TIME has effaced what he has done,
    The course of life that he had run:
Sinful or good, ah! who can say
Lies there the last of human clay?
What he had done and how he died
Were once upon that stone espied,
And there he made his final bed,
And there was laid his icy head;
No more can now be seen or said
    Over this graveyard wide.

A solemn silence reigns around
That speaks of this as hallowed ground;
Many the tears that once were shed—
Home of the now forgotten dead.
Flowers and plants have faded all,
Graves are ruined and tombstones fall;
Distant echoes lisp in the air,
Solemnly seeming to declare—
The bones of men are buried there:
    And yet no spirits call.

———··><··——— —

A KISSING GOOD-BYE AND A SIGHING FAREWELL.

WHEN last we were parted how bitter our tears
    As they flowed from the depths of the heart;
The bonds of affection which rapt us for years
    Could recoil not to have us thus part.
We clung but in vain and our dreamings we feared,
    Of the moments, oh, how can I tell?
I was dumb when her quivering lips were heard
    To be kissing good-bye and sighing farewell;
Her beautiful voice ev'ry pang in me stirred
    While kissing good-bye and while sighing farewell.

I gazed on her face that with sorrow was pale,
  But the tears were too thick in mine eyes;
The beats of my heart you could hear like a flail,
  And my breast like a billow did rise.
Few words did we speak; we were stifled for speech;
  With a struggle our spirits they fell,
For joy hastened from us, evading our reach
  While kissing good-bye and while sighing farewell:
We were frenzied with grief while passing to each
  A kissing good-bye and a sighing farewell.

LOVE.

THE best of affections, of passions is Love,
  Sent down unto man from Elysium above;
Sent down unto him just to comfort his breast
If the cares of the world e'er trouble his rest;
To soothe away sorrow, to lend him a glow
That will shine on his path where'er he may go;
To spare him sweet friendship, the pleasures of hope,
Though with storms and troubles through life he may
    cope.
Oh, who such a blessing would trifle and shun,
Which Nature herself has bestowed on each one?
Surely man would not plume his bosom with pride,
And the heaven-sent bounty lay careless aside?

Around as he views ev'ry scene is of love,
The green turf beneath him, the planets above;
The birds that melodiously chant in the air,
The sweetest of choristers known anywhere:
The brooks that run softly, the cascades that fall,
The light lingering zephyrs that reign over all.
Oh, Love, pure and gentle, though harmless yet warm,
How oft hast thou driven to silence a storm:
Oh, fill my poor breast, give me nectar like thine,
Give me something which I may claim only as mine,
For truly I know as by flowers I rove—
Unhappy's the heart that partakes not of love.

ON THE "DEVIL DANCE" COLLECTION.

In the Museum, Cinnamon Gardens, Colombo.

WITH all that Western culture can impart,
    And British rule command with pow'r perforce,
        These witless men will follow on their own course,
By worshipping the dread satanic art.
Behold collected here—it makes one start—
        Agony depicted from ev'ry source.

Behold those masks bedaubed with horrid paint,
    That put to shame the knowledge we are men ;
Those semblances are not what we call quaint,
    But the product of imagination when
It finds no rest and bears with it the taint
        Of Hades' darkest den,
Where ghouls and fiends with visage such as these
Must shriek with pain, swept by the flaming seas
        That toss them o'er again.

Aye, some have sorrows much as they can bear,
And others have it in a greater share ;
But watch that face and tell me if you please,
        If ever you have known
        In all that's flesh and bone,
Contortions such as those in that disease ?
The red, the brown, the yellow, and the green,
    That black—ah, does it make the bosom throb ?
The inartistic brush too prodigal has been
    And shocks one's taste with its unearthly daub.

'Tis said of old upon a Grecian isle,
    An artist burnt with irons a guiltless boy,
    So that a greater fame he might enjoy
In painting misery with uncommon guile :
While great Angelo, following up the style,
    A slave had bought and crucified,
        That he might better know
        The deepest, direst woe
In which a hapless mortal died.

Disgraceful means! Can genius not discern
   What since Creation common fate has wrought?
   Or glean from painful sights that come unsought,
Reminding us that these are men we spurn?
Can genius not from scenes that shame us learn,
   Giving us things that be, not as they ought?

But here a race revere the devil-god,
   And partly following Buddha's moral teaching,
Fear more the evil pow'r on ev'ry clod
Their feet from early infancy have trod,
   And ever, in all circumstance beseeching.
Misguided souls! Thou wantest not the rod,
But while the Christian elders 'mong thee plod,
   More zeal and tact in missionary preaching.

SONNET: RAPTURE.

A THOUGHT—a hope—a dream! Ah, what is this
   That overtakes me now and fills my breast?
   I feel within a spirit roused from rest,
As every cord that binds it bursts amiss.
As fire volcanic from some dark abyss,
   In ebullition; or as one possessed—
So do I feel within. And is this bliss?
   In feeling such sure one cannot be blest?
There is a sensibility in such,
Of truth but little, of deception much,
   Which 'cutely blinds the vision of our eyes,
And gives a death-like numbness to the touch.
Aye, this *is* rapture what ye name: but know
Behind it stands the shadow of dark woe;
   And ere we count the time the former flies.

WHO WOULD HAVE THOUGHT OF THEE?

SPEAK not those words; they break my heart,
   They tear all joy from me;
How could I wish from thee to part
   When love in thee I see?
"Who would have thought of thee," my love?
   Oh! sad and grieved is me;
I swear by all the stars above—
   I would have thought of thee.
         The world is vain
         Without thy strain:
I would have thought of thee.

When pain and anguish sought my head,
   And fever took my brain,
When sickness chained me to my bed—
   Thou turned to me in pain.
I saw thy breast for me did move,
   Thy pity I did see;
And wouldst thou say, my precious love,
   "Who would have thought of thee?"
         Forget me not,
         I'll share thy lot,
For I must think of thee.

Here is my hand, here is my heart,
   Deal with them as you would;
Fear not, thy mind to me impart,
   True love they say is good.
I see the smile dawn on thy cheek,
   I know it is for me;
Nought can impede the love I speak,
   For I must think of thee.
         Then smile again,
         It soothes all pain
Whilst I bethink of thee.

TO A HANDSOME YOUNG LADY,

Seen on the Port Melbourne Pier one early Morning.

WHY dost thou with thy little brother on the quay
    Wait at this hour, when 'tis scarce six at morn?
Perhaps a lover comes from o'er the sea,
    And in his absence thou dost feel forlorn.
And yet thy look perplexes me again,
    I long from thine own lips to hear the truth,
For Nature's favoured child thou'rt surely when
She gives thee what are most admired by men—
    Virtue and loveliness and creamy youth.
Yet why that anxious gaze?   No sail appears
    Out in the distance thus to give thee hope :
Is this alone thy grief in tender years,
    With nought besides in lovely youth to cope?
Then thou art blest : may be thy lover hies,
    Anxious as e'er to clasp thee in his arms ;
May be on deck he now with wistful eyes,
Marks the direction in which Melbourne lies ;
    And won't he find thee in thy loveliest charms?

ON THE DEATH OF ACANTHA.

OH, lost for ever, turned to dust
    When in thine happiest bloom ;
In heav'n alone was placed thy trust,
    Hence flees thy soul so soon.
And must I now be left behind,
With none to cheer my aching mind,
    Thou angel now—no lass?
Ah! why so mocks the fleeting wind?
    Alas! alas! alas!

I feel the ever-flowing tear
　　Now gushing to mine eyes;
Oh, that I knew that thou dost hear
　　My pleadings from the skies.
A love so old, a life so young,
Music was in thy virgin tongue,
　　From which no ill did pass:
Once with the fondest hopes I clung—
　　But now alas! alas!

————————⊷✕⊶————————

OH, SING YOUR SONGS AGAIN.

'TWAS oft I heard your voice in youth,
　　My thoughts it did instil;
I softly crept to hear its truth,
　　And me with rapture fill.
But silent now it is to me,
　　Its each familiar strain;
I nigh forget its melody,
　　Then sing your songs again.

Shall I not hear the gentle voice
　　That springs with tuneful lay,
That makes the weary heart rejoice,
　　And takes all grief away?
The bloom that rests upon thy cheek
　　Removes the tragic pain;
Oh, then, fair maid, arise and speak,
　　And sing your songs again.

Light as the sylph those tones shall fly
　　And mingle with the air;
What harp retains or could supply
　　The chords secluded there?
Sweet Philomel does sit the bough
　　His voice to tune in vain:
Then cherished maid, why silent thou?—
　　Oh, sing your songs again.

DEAREST FLO.

DEAREST Flo, for thy sake I have pondered too long,
  Mine eyes now appear as in mist;
The pure feeling of love in my breast is so strong,
  Its tide I can never resist.
My heart it would crumble and my spirit would fail,
  Each moment of anguish would be—
If thou bid me to never look on thee again,
  Or never to more think of thee.
If thou bid me go hence and sail over the foam,
  The sweets all around thee forsake,
I would go, but in dreams I would think thee mine own,
  And cry to the last when awake.

Thy fair face is the sun that illumines my days,
  Smiles, blushes, and gladness are there;
Surely Nature has lavished the works of her praise
  To make thee a jewel so rare.
On thy lips there is music so gentle and sweet;
  There is poetry within thine eyes,
And the flash of their look is so harmless yet fleet,
  While blushes upon thee arise.
Oh! do give me thine heart, pure as regions above,
  Its loss I could never survive;
Dearest Flo, do but pity the slave of thy love,
  If thou wouldst but have me alive.

— —•••••—

'TWAS A MOMENT.

'TWAS a moment I dwelt on that beautiful face,
  'Twas a moment I gazed on its charms,
'Twas a moment alone and I quickly did trace
  All the joy that a youthful heart warms.
In a moment I knew I could love you for e'er,
  In a moment was struck with a dart;
It was Cupid who shot it direct through the air,
  In a moment 'twas plunged in my heart.

'Twas a moment you stood and you heard the deep sigh,
　'Twas a moment you looked to the ground;
In a moment you caught ev'ry glance of mine eye
　In a moment you blushed and you frowned;
In a moment I summoned all courage to speak,
　In a moment knelt down at thy shrine;
In a moment thy love ever sacred did seek,
　In a moment you said you were mine.

ON SOLICITATION.

Verses written at the end of a Scrap Album.

OH, now for those pleasures in caves of locked treasures,
　We seek in our leisures for the future in store;
Where sweet Philomel's voice with his ballads of choice
　Makes our bosoms rejoice and enchants to the core:
Where sweets of the season crowd the varying year,
The peer and the peasant meet the very same cheer—
Oh, thither transplant me; I don't wish to stay here
　　　　　　　　　　Any more.

Each thought has transition to regions Elysian,
　E'en the world in a vision beholds its decay;
All hopes have departed, success has been thwarted,
　And now broken-hearted pining here shall I stay?
Better far than earth's joys is the peace of the vault,
Where no power has man to demean or exalt;
For here cynics will scorn and vain critics find fault
　　　　　　　　　　Ev'ry day.

Still one comfort remains, one sole joy 'mid my pains,
　As I lift up the chains which dear friendship has wrought,
The one smile it bestows drives the frown of my woes,
　So calmly I close the scrapbook I have brought.
You have seen, perhaps, things which are both old and
　　new,
Which are getting more common or rare to the view;
And if faults here you find let me then question you—
　　　　　　　　　　Who has not?

HIS LAST GOOD-BYE.

THE vessel lay upon the foam,
　　And on the rugged reef
Brave Hal and I stood all alone,
　　And sighed and sobbed in grief.
In vain I tried amidst my woe
To speak a parting word, for, oh!
　　I knew his stay was brief.
The day was then declining fast,
　　And tears poured from his eye;
He took my hand and bade at last
　　" Farewell"—his last good-bye.

Next time I heard of Hal was when
　　By post he sent a note;
He said he had no ink nor pen,
　　So with a pencil wrote.
Those lines to me are ever dear,
I kiss them hundred times or near;
　　On them I ever dote.
And these were his last words to me—
　　" My love, pray do not cry;
Some day I may return to thee;
　　At present, dear, good-bye."

A battle has been fought, I'm told,
　　The day by us was won;
And many wounded lay, or cold
　　In death, the field upon.
But dreadful news came o'er the sea,
That Hal would not return to me,
　　That he from earth was gone.
But in the last of what was life
　　They heard him gently cry—
" Good-bye to you, my darling wife:"
　. It was his last good-bye.

FLOWERS.

At an Agri-Horticultural Exhibition.

BEAUTIFUL flow'rs all spangled with dew,
Fresh-gathered and rich in the splendours of hue;
Spreading thy fragrance around ev'rywhere,
From places of vantage arranged by the fair,
In clusters and posies all trimmed with such care,
That eye seeks in vain which track to pursue,
Encompassed with beauties perplexing the view.

Ye bright-tinted flow'rs, in growth and in form
Dividing the charms which thy presence adorn,
Each with an attraction entirely its own;
Your many reflections for ever have shown
How Nature herself lives unrivalled, alone;
That the artist is false, and there never was born
Who could liken thy sleeping or picture thy morn.

Ye sweet-smelling flow'rs, we clasp thee with pride,
Our tokens of love, peace and friendship beside;
We gather thee fondly and breathe of thy spell,
We use thee our tenderest passions to tell,
To comfort the sick or their fearings to quell:
We strew thee with joy at the feet of the bride,
And lay thee with rev'rence on those who have died.

Ye earth-blessing flow'rs, I've breathed of thy charms,
From the morning of life to my true lover's arms;
I find thee e'er cheering wherever I roam,
A comfort 'mid strangers, a blessing at home,
A treasure to contemplate when I'm alone;
And the gems here now gathered—how mem'ry embalms
All their emblems of love and their light-winged alarms.

LOVE'S VICTORY.

OH, if my spirit breathes a purer air,
  Or feels a charm that must illume the face—
It is when certain I am of a share
  Of thy chaste love, and in its holy place
  Find all the qualities that woman grace.
United hearts have countless bliss in store,
  They lose the world and brighter planets trace;
Therefore I wish to thee alone adore,
And winning thee, behold with thee a brighter shore.

Say was there not a time when strangers we
  Secluded dwelt, without a thought of love?
But Time's assiduous hand strew flow'rs o'er thee,
  And tell-tale zephyrs led thee to the grove.
  Then was my heart in flame, my breast did move,
To curious consciousness my senses woke.
  The friendship formed with passion quickly strove,
And in a sweet short hour the truth I spoke—
I said I loved thee, and the secret then was broke.

Yes, but you spoke not, and it made me fear;
  A pang had drawn within its unseen gore,
As if some aerial ghoul had cast his spear,
  Which in its plunging first essayed the core.
  My nerves relaxed; the life blood now no more
Exultant ran; and pale my visage grew.
  Oh! it was dreadful, pitiful and sore;
I did not mean to trifle nor pursue
A course dishonourable, or speak one word untrue.

Yes, still you spoke not: ah! and why the dread?
  Did you my ardent words then disbelieve?
Did you a moment scorn what I had said,
  And flushed with anger turn aside to leave?
  Remorse filled me the while; my heart did grieve,
No sinner was so penitent as I;
  But words we can't recall, nor time retrieve;
'Tis better to explain ourselves than fly,
To breathe in hope and live than to despondent die.

While in a meditative mood, with upturned eyes,
　　I saw a tim'rous smile upon thee dawn ;
Then was the time to win or lose the prize,
　　The purest heart that e'er for man was born,
　　That gives to life its own peculiar morn.
Say, did not gentler feelings move thee then,
　　To look less archly on poor me forlorn,
Standing in painful agitation when
One word would make most blest the wretchedest of men ?

You asked me what I meant ; I spoke again,
　　With fervour more ; your lips did scarcely move :
My earnest tears I strove to hide in vain ;
　　Could you then disregard or doubt my love ?
　　Nay, in thy nature 'twas not to reprove;
Thy mingling tears then chased each other down ;
　　All-pitying heav'n whispered from above—
" Thus we unite two hearts, and thus we crown
With happiness the pair who mutual love have shown."

Let us consider how our future may
　　Glide with the hours that crowd the life of each ;
And scatter flowers at the dawn of day,
　　To bless the eve and bring within our reach
　　Love, faith, sincerity and simple speech.
With these our own the world can we defy,
　　And silence rumours and our foes dismay ;
For there are people with the jaundiced eye
Who live to scandalise and give to truth the lie.

Why should they dare molest with idle words
　　The unoffending victims of their pride ;
And flock together like the unclaimed herds
　　That are run down but for their flesh and hide ;
　　Or sport to the bold huntsman and his pack provide?
Envy's the canker worm that slowly eats within
　　The brambles when all other plants have died;
It finds in virtue but the mask of sin,
And feels its poverty when others' joys begin.

My beauteous maid, my own devoted one,
  Thou wilt not this my simple lay reprove ;
And now thy heart that I at last have won,
  Nothing can add to overflowing love.
  And this I vow by all the pow'rs above—
Of mine what's earthly all to thee belong.
  Oh, let not jealousy thy passions move :
With hearts united, unity is strong,
And with no secrets 'tween us ne'er can we do wrong.

THE HOMELESS MOTHER AND HER DYING CHILD.

(An Incident in Melbourne, Christmas Eve, 1891.)

ALL Christendom tendered its greetings,
  All people were joyous and gay,
Wherever were partings and meetings,
  Each one had a kind word to say.
The old and the young joined together,
  'Twas a time for no sadness to be,
For the toiler had broke from his tether,
  And the master had bid him go free.
Oh, man ! in this time of our pleasure
Shall we count up our years and then measure
What we've won, what we've left of our treasure,
  How the balance stands 'twixt you and me ?

Of toil shall we think any longer,
  Before '91 runs its course ?
How this holiday makes one feel stronger,
  And talk on without feeling hoarse.
Your wine is a good appetiser,
  Yes, thanks, I don't mind another ;
Quite sure I won't be a late riser,
  Or have with my head any bother.
At Christmas we're always good creatures,
Hospitality's best of our features,
And we'll list to the dullest of preachers,
  And all our grievances smother.

E

You say how the years they are fleeting,
   And that we are both getting old ;
Well, what's that to do with our treating
   Each other as come of one fold ?
We've seen many days such as this is,
   Festive seasons like this come and go;
And in these our short-living blisses,
   We've forgot each long-continued woe.
Merry Christmas to you! Many others
May we see ; with our wives and our mothers,
Our children, our sisters, our brothers,
   May the cup of fortune o'erflow.

Gay throngs in the streets are out shopping,
   The shops make their grandest display;
Blithe children each moment are stopping,
   To wish they could take all away.
What feasting there'll be on the morrow,
   Rejoicings on land and the main;
Good-bye to all rancour and sorrow
   While music and happiness reign.
Plum pudding and roast beef as of old,
And turkey and goose and best of fruits sold,
Shall our tables with flow'rs and foliage hold,
   For Christmas has come round again.

'Twas Christmas eve and all the world was gay,
While a poor woman hurried on her way,
   Carrying a dying child.
She scarcely knew whither she onward went,
But being impelled in that predicament,
   Distracted too and wild,
On one sole purpose were her thoughts intent:
"Oh, God! My child unto me spare,
My God, my God, this is my earnest pray'r!
I've nothing left, this is my only care,
   My infant undefiled.
The world will not with me its treasures share,
But take not from me this in my despair,
   And I am reconciled:
I want not else, my sorrow I can bear.

I ask no more I solemnly declare,
Than this my babe, so innocent and fair—
My own, my darling child!"

Onward she hurried; in the distance gleamed
The city's lights invitingly: nor dreamed
She that in all the ills she must deplore,
This heartless world had sorrows still in store.
Her cup was full she thought, the flow must stop,
But had not reckoned on the one last drop
That quickens all the rest and leaves no hope
To those who with adversity must cope.
Onward she went, scarce turning either side,
While still those lights before her she descried—
The lights of Melbourne, and their lambent gleam
That distance gives the outline of a dream;
The circling mist that settles from above,
The shadows that with deeper shadows move.
Past her the cabs and coaches rattled on,
As if a purse, a cup, was to be won,
And cheerful chatt'ring folk of ev'ry age,
Sharpened their wits in pleasure to engage.
Laughter the merriest, sounds of joy and cheers,
From near and all around fell on her ears;
But heedless quite of all, she heard alone,
No more affected than the sculptured stone,
And hurried onward still, though faint and sore,
Clinging with tend'rest care the babe she bore.
Fold after fold her shawl she round it wove,
Kissed it, embraced it with a mother's love;
Its fitful moaning and its feeble cry
Met her responsive throbs and painful sigh;
None looked at them, nor did she feel concerned
While one sole thought her brain, her being burned —
'Twas for her child; she felt that she could give
Anything, ev'rything to have it live;
Nought else remained to her; her life a blank,
She for compassion had no one to thank;
The world was nothing to her; and she knew
None but her child as closer still she drew

Its tender form unto her aching breast,
Whisp'ring sweet words and lulling it to rest.

How long those moments seemed, how slow they flew,
Heavy the night air, dull and mocking too;
How she the city reached she could not tell;
With whirling brain and swollen eyes as well,
She did not pause to think; a moment lost
Might mean for her incalculable cost;
Till with a trembling hand she stood and knocked
At a large iron gate; 'twas firmly locked.
Hospital? Yes; the dreary spot she knew,
The watchman queries and then lets her through;
Into the building hurries she, relieved;
Nay, 'tis not so; 'tis but to be deceived;
The cruel shock—no room, no beds to spare;
Spurned from the doors, into the midnight air
She turns again, shelter elsewhere to find,
Some refuge more hospitably inclined.
Her steps retraced, but reeling 'neath that blow,
Unchristian treatment—where was she to go?
O'ercome at last, she rests upon the way,
Broken in health, but striving still to pray;
It might have been an hour, may be 'twas more,
She rested there, upon earth's stony floor;
Till feeling better—and how little too—
She rose again her journey to pursue.
But disappointment met her ev'rywhere,
More cruel shocks—no room, no beds to spare;
No home for her, none for her dying child;
The world was large, but Fortune never smiled
On unfortunates helpless such as they,
So they must go unnoticed on their way.

Dawn broke at last, and it was Christmas morn,
While a poor child unto the morgue was borne;
It was that mother's child: unseen there came
The angels on the Saviour's day to claim
That spotless soul, to be no more of earth,
But join with them for aye in heav'nly mirth,
And sing in choir upon the Saviour's birth.

AUSTRALIA'S FOURTH ESTATE.

HOW changed the world's from what our fathers knew,
  Its manners altered and opinions too ;
Arts, manufactures, trades of ev'ry kind
Have aided to enlarge the human mind ;
And progress still in ev'ry prospect glows,
And man in knowledge fast his age outgrows.
The civilising influences around
Have for his genius new inventions found,
To add to comfort and console his breast,
And pleasures yield his fathers ne'er possessed.
So will succeeding generations find
That they have left us fairly far behind,
And with their newer knowledge doubtless cast
A look of scorn or pity on the past.

However this, whatever bliss was known
To ancient Greece or Rome's imperial throne,
Whatever luxuries were daily stored
To grace the Eastern monarch's festive board—
They still were beings of inferior mould,
Those kings, those princes, and those men of old.
The world moved round them, deeds of daring done,
Actions diverse from rise to set of sun ;
Great incidents which issues grave involved,
Were caused and ended, problems weighty solved ;
Thrones toppled o'er, empires were swept away,
Events alluring marked out ev'ry day :
Yet more than half the world oblivious lived,
Unconscious how the rest in purpose thrived ;
News travelled slow for want of printers' orders,
And slower still beyond their native borders.
No morning journals graced their tables then,
No ev'ning print was bawled by boys and men ;
The wholesome sheet of current news was ne'er
Known to patrician or proletaire.

Their news was gossip, and their gossip grew,
As mouth to mouth and round the town it flew;
And while 'twas so, while this neglect remained,
And none his daily journal had obtained,
Man's intellect remained in sorry plight,
His finer instincts were uncultured quite;
He groped in darkness for the news he sought,
Electric currents were beyond his thought;
Cables nor post, nor printers' ink nor steam,
E'er found a fragment in his wildest dream.

Time was when gagging journals were in force,
And rogues impeached rejoiced, although, of course,
They smarted 'neath the strictures of the pen,
Not those of foes, but Britain's truest men.
In England first they had the *Weekly News*,
But leading articles came not in use
Till Swift, Defoe and Bolingbroke gave life
Anew in lampoons, Parliamentary strife.
Years came and fled, and journals lived and died,
Still, as in spite, the journals multiplied;
And, at this day, though few of them survive,
Others from them a newer life derive:
On past experience and on modern growth
Of skill, they thrive, and yet improve on both.
An ev'ning journal London then produced,
The public liked the stranger introduced;
And as from toil homewards they meandered,
Each bought a copy of that ev'ning's *Standard*.

With but one bound o'er thousand leagues of foam,
Let us approach our own Australian home;
The land of glorious harvests, and the clime
That charms both young and old and those in prime,
Who, starting fresh adventures, cry " Behold!
Here plough or plant, here build or sink for gold."
But in this life's commotion we possess,
The first-born of the great Australian Press
Saw light before those beauteous streams and shore,
Which bring back fancies of our fairy lore;

Where midst her scenes that mem'ry e'er embalms,
Historic Sydney boasts superior charms.
Tasmania followed with her *Derwent Star*,
" A paper?" asked the fair one ; " There you are."
It roared and spluttered with sulphurous breath,
And, fed on scandal, soon was choked to death.

Now let us pause, for tread we on that soil
Where heroes wrenched success by arduous toil ;
And, like true Britons, scarce had settled down
Within their shanties, which they called a town,
When 'twas devised—what jokes their ghosts could
    crack—
To start a cricket club—now comes the smack—
Also a journal—and we wonder whether
Their news was new, or extracts strung together.
Well, this first infant was a great surpriser,
Styled pompously the *Melbourne Advertiser* ;
The staff their pens in blackish liquid dipped,
And sent their bantling forth in manuscript,
Till disused type came round in ocean ships,
And these in time were worn to very strips.

Lo! how the scene has changed, the world behold ;
The Press Australian in its wisdom old,
Leaps to the front to toe in line with those
Of older growth, stern giant scribes of prose.
Who can foretell what may be still in store ;
Inventive genius bids us look for more ;
Yea ; and while men for news and knowledge live,
The more they'll prize the more the Press can give.
From rough-hewn hand machines that moved with groans
And oft broke down or broke the workman's bones—
The Press has onward marched, resolved to gain
The brightest talent money can obtain ;
Wielding a pow'r so formed to explicate,
That nations stared, then hailed a Fourth Estate.

BUILDING CASTLES IN THE AIR.

POOR worn-out heart, dejection seems thy lot,
    E'en airy trifles seem to worry thee ;
Thou art too sensitive ; hast thou forgot
    Man from his ills can draw felicity ?

I own thy burden none would care to bear ;
    Thy face thy troubles has this e'er confessed ;
But where's the mortal, canst thou tell me where,
    Who through all seasons feels that he is blest ?

When I know that I'm forsaken by Fortuna and her train,
    Then a misty cloud comes o'er me and my breast is
        steeped in care ;
But a moment, and I ponder—why in health should I
        complain ?
    Let me peer into the future and build castles in the air.

Let me understand myself and try to know that things
        must change ;
    Light and shade together mingle, parting now and
        meeting there ;
Joy and sorrow each succeeding in a moment seeming
        strange,
    So, in sorrow know joy follows, and build castles in
        the air.

When my fevered brow was aching and my pulse had
        beat apace,
    Helpless lay my hands beside me, with mine eyes in
        glossy glare ;
But the kind words of a few friends and their sympathetic
        grace,
    Helped me more than gold could purchase to build
        castles in the air.

In my youth when knowing little of the world that lay
  before me,
  And giving nought to reason of the paths I'd have to
    dare,
Save that all were beds of roses, with no evils to come
    o'er me,
  Then I'd watch the stars at nightfall and build castles
    in the air.

Noisy shouts and madsome gambols, and at times a
    scene of strife,
  Marked the lawn where after study we would hurriedly
    repair;
It was then youth's daily carnival, the heyday of our life,
  And on the turf I'd lie when wearied, to build castles
    in the air.

At night still further study—but an hour in speedy flight;
  Then four hundred voices blended in sweet hymn and
    solemn pray'r;
But mine eyes refused their closing till long 'twas past
    midnight,
  For I'd plan a long existence filled with castles in the air.

How things have all reversed themselves, both in order
    and in time;
  And launched just on the sea of life, ah, must not one
    despair?
Recoiling at each venture as if my boyhood was a crime,
  I would homeward wend at evetide to build castles
    in the air.

Disappointment! thou inglorious fiend of countless crimes
    and evils,
  Dashing all our hopes and fancies on the barren rock
    —Despair;
Why so haunt us with your creatures, the worst of unseen
    devils,
  And scoff and scorn and laugh at all our castles in the
    air?

Spite of thee and thy dominion, spite of thee and all
 thine host,
 Still defy will I thy pow'r, for I fear it not nor care;
I've regained in untold treasures what on earth I may
 have lost,
 Just by building and re-building mighty castles in the
 air.

I will pluck the choicest flow'rs, bind me laurel wreaths
 each morn,
 Carol on my toilsome journey though the paths lead
 ev'rywhere;
Maze nor mist shall give me terror, as man's heritage
 here born,
 As men have done before me I'll build castles in the
 air.

Pain nor anguish shall deprive me of the dreams I've
 loved to dream,
 Misfortune too shall know that I have strength her
 fangs to bear;
Be my station e'er so lowly, it will be my constant theme
 Of joy that knows no limit—building castles in the air.

Then I've gold and countless riches, and a mansion,
 park, and hounds,
 And a crowd of proud retainers, who disloyalty for-
 swear;
And I listen to the songs of birds and the sweetly
 plaintive sounds
 Of swans that glide upon the lake by my castles in
 the air.

I hear my children prattle, while she who my heart does
 share
 Is busy at her toilet, and she looks divinely fair:
She scarce has put her bonnet on, when up drives the
 chaise and pair,
 'Neath the portal of the castle I have built up in the
 air.

Thus busied on I have through life, building castles
    ev'rywhere,
  Parks and gardens now are seen on lands once desolate
    and bare ;
Till there seems scarce further room for me, scarce ten
    square yards to spare,
  But I'll pull down older ones for newer castles in the
    air.

ALGIERS.

LUMINOUS, bright with sunshine, tow'ring high,
  And spread above a most congenial sky,
The famous mountain city, cone-like formed,
By gallant Blake menaced, by Exmouth stormed,
Now stays in calm possession of the Gaul,
Yet stocked with cannon foemen to appal.
Our vessel glides, her engines almost cease,
Her mission's one of commerce and of peace,
But as she enters port, on ev'ry side
Conspicuous rears the Gallic martial pride.
On ev'ry hand the bristling guns agape,
Show readiness from shore to shore and cape ;
While right before, frowning, and fierce and grim,
Yet with her ordnance all in glossy trim,
That island stands a sentinel alway,
A threat, a warning both by night and day.

  How Time works wonders, how the place has changed,
And things by diff'rent laws and means arranged ;
Algiers, the terror once upon the foam,
The desperadoes' haunt, the pirates' home,
Swarming with human devils, fiends who bore
Their craft abroad for treasure and for gore—
Now garners her resources, and her page
Of history forms a marvel of the age.

The swarthy Moor has found himself displaced,
The Arab from his stronghold has been chased;
Their madsome orgies and their midnight brawls,
Their untold vices in their gairish halls,
Their shouts of vengeance 'gainst the Christian world,
Their Christian captives into dungeons hurled—
Have led to their discomfiture and fall,
While now they see the polished, cultured Gaul
Trip with assurance through their narrow streets,
Walk with the fair or bow to her he meets;
Pull down their terraces with age o'ergrown,
And with more elegance erect his own;
Displace their fondues and their coffee stalls,
For squares and stately homes and gorgeous halls;
While the Jardin Marengo—favoured spot!
Bright perennial beauty is her lot—
Loads the soft zephyrs through the changing hours
With scents delicious of her varied flow'rs.

There blooms the sweet pomegranate, and beside
The lovely aloe flourishes in pride;
The wealth of tropic soil takes kindly there,
And all is beautiful and all is fair.
Vineyards and olive groves surround the scene,
And honest toil where roguery had been,
Gladdens the soul of him who takes his stand
Upon some slope and watches o'er the land.
Terrace above terrace, house above house,
Lo, their ascent one's fancy doth arouse;
So on, above a thousand feet they rise,
Like Babel's tow'r to wrestle with the skies.
And, as you upward climb—Oh, glorious sight!
More than the pen of mortal can indite;
Surpassing beauty meets at ev'ry turn,
Nature in newer aspects you discern;
The sapphire-tinted ocean, same as yore,
Bears not the ruthless craft of eld she bore,
But floating luxuries, to peace allied,
That come and go e'er buoyant with the tide;
Declaring to the world the triumph won
O'er wildest state barbaric 'neath the sun.

How Europe shiv'rs now in all her snows,
Her sky o'ercast, her streams lulled to repose;
The fogs of London, thick'ning with the hour,
Becloud St. Paul's and screen from view the Tow'r;
In academic Fleet-street and the Strand,
Men grope their way or in confusion stand,
And when we anchor weighed and left behind
The crowded docks, how was our course defined ?—
To landsmen 'twas a mystery that grew,
How the good skipper got his bearings through.
Lo, sun-wrapt Algiers, how a few days' sail
Changes the scene, the burden of one's tale ;
And ev'ry ship in this most wintry weather,
From distant lands due warmth to seek together,
Brings mortals frail, who fleeing from the snows,
The bitter cold and its attendant woes,
Find here retreat, a clime they can endure,
A temporary home, serene, secure.

December, 1875.

————·>I<····   —

THE MEETING OF THE TROOPSHIPS.

[Her Majesty's Troopship *Jumna*, which left Portsmouth on 11th
October, 1885, when one day's sail from Bombay harbour, on
the 8th of the following month, passed H.M.S. *Malabar*, which
stopped and took on letters for relatives and friends in the
United Kingdom.]

" ADIEU !" was the cry as they cast from the pier,
        In affection they ne'er were so open and true;
And while the taut vessel to vision was clear,
    The cry was the same, it was "Farewell!" "Adieu!"
Farewell to the brave, who from loved ones and home,
Who from instincts of duty for country and Queen,

Left the land of their fathers, whose standard has flown
   O'er realms they scarce heard of and never had seen.
Moist eyes from the vessel, moist eyes from the beach,
Gazed and fancied the loved ones most loved unto each,
   Till the picture resembled a dream.

On sailed the proud trooper, and many a sail
   Peeped o'er the horizon, like a phantom at night,
Knowing nought of the stranger whom no one could hail,
   Who could say but a sail indistinct was in sight.
But at eve mellow music, and dancing and song
   To day's gloomy broodings and sorrows gave flight;
And at morn ev'ry eye would be tracing along,
   For land, where the sky and the ocean unite.
But a day still remains and the voyage is o'er,
But a day to write home they've reached safely the shore,
   When, "Ho!" goes the cry, "There's a trooper in
      sight!"

What commotion prevails while all clamber on deck,
   Or from larboard and starboard below seek a glance;
For the news is too true, and their joy knows no check,
   While the two gallant troopers right welcome advance.
Then the ship seems deserted awhile, for each one
   Returns to his cabin in hurry to tell
The loved ones at home how the voyage was done,
   And ask of the loved ones if they are all well.
'Tis the work of a moment; and the vessels bear on;
For the anxious and absent a day has been won;
   And the whole thing resembles a spell.

THE PLEASURES OF DREAMING.

"A Dream itself is but a Shadow."—*Shakespeare.*

THE ARGUMENT.

The question put forth.—Memory.—The woeful appearances of men.—Sleep.—What is a dream?—Juvenile expectations.—The joy occasioned on awakening after a frightful dream.—The days primeval.—Hellas: A retrospect of its mythology.—Rome.—The continuation of dreams from infancy to manhood.—The lover's dream.—Dreams do not always prove to be fallacious: they are sometimes omens.—The dreams of poets.—Shakespeare.—Milton.—Otway and Jonson.—Swift and Addison.—Goldsmith.—Savage and Chatterton.—The mariner: his fond recollections and sweet delusions.—The soldier forgets his agonies in sleep and pictures the delights of home.—A moral reflection.

HY weeps this eye? Why heaves this
mortal breast?
Is there no soothing balm to give me rest?
Is there no cheering mem'ry of the past
To solace breathe and make me blest at last?
To me this life is as a pretty flow'r,
That smiles at sunshine, yielding to a show'r,
And while partaking of the liquid store,
Closes its leaves as if those joys are sore ;
Yet fresher rises when the clouds have fled,
With fragrant zephyrs playing round its head.
Death is the same to me : 'tis like the hand
That culls the various flowers of the land ;
Leaving but wretched traces where they grew
In all the beauty of their brilliant hue.
Oh, ye who ease your limbs on beds of down,
Far from the jangled tumults of the town,
Where cries discordant never tease the ear,
To have your blithesome fancyings disappear—
Where is the covert that ye fain would gain,
In realms remote, beyond the angry main,
If sorrow closed its curtains round your forms,
Or in your breast made havoc by its storms?
Where is the spot ye would select on earth?
On lands afar, the cradle of your birth;

The distant islet circled by the waves,
The world of waters or the world of graves;
The glorious East that fascinates the eye,
Or bitter winds that sweep a Northern sky?
Which, can ye tell? Your voice for e'er is mute,
The pang of disappointment is acute;
You dare not speak that one ideal joy
Whose absence serves all patience to destroy.

Oh, ye in penury born, who lie at ease
On beds of hay or 'neath the woodland trees,
Where would ye fly, ah, where on earth below,
To shun the rigours of all brutal woe?
How can ye pass away from such a gloom?
Yet in the lands around is there no room?
No distant voice that bids ye come away,
And live to see the dawn of brighter day?
Hark! but the wish is false, the thought is vain;
Sorrow pursues with her amorphous train,
And Disappointment staring from the eyes,
Palsies each nerve and bids the shades arise,
Heaps woe on woe till mystifying the whole,
Man circumvented is of all control.

There is no need to change thy dwelling-place,
Nor view the faces of a stranger race;
Remember, though familiar scenes are left,
And those endeared by time from thee are cleft,
Memory, that spirit, speaks within the mind,
And through it bliss, or all our woes, we find.
It tells of years that would have been forgot,
Relates of youth and each sequestered spot;
Aids in a task that would an adage give,
For well it knoweth how a heart might live:
It knows no dread, and while impartial clad,
Whispers our actions be they good or bad.
There is but one appeaser of the soul,
That gently draws beneath its sweet control
The fleeting hours of each successive day,
When sombre hues conceal the solar ray;
When planets move within their ether deep,
It loves to come, and it is known as SLEEP.

Balm of the soul! Thou precious gift of heav'n,
Sleep! let the pangs that torture me be driv'n,
Hurled from the shores so thronged with men aghast,
Who fear their future and bewail their past.
Behold their faces, pale with bitter dread,
Which seem not of the living but the dead;
Observe their forms that totter as they go,
Observe their breasts that flutter to and fro,
The meagre flesh, the eyes all sunken low;
Lo, on their brows what furrows mark along,
Their lips to murmur prone, but never song.
And, can they censure thee for ev'ry ill?
Oh, Somnus, hast thou fled or reigning still?
Yet dost thou feed ambrosia to the eyes,
And hush from out the breast its thousand sighs?
At morn or eve, say when is thy best hour,
When dost thou rule with autocratic power?—
When dewdrops fall and Cynthia shows her light,
And silence broods at intermediate night.

Aye, in my cherished home I feel thee bless
My wearied heart, my drooping eyelids press;
I know the happy solace of thy breath,
Thy silent form so close allied to death;
And fast my sorrows flee, ill-humours fade,
While Pleasure comes in all the flow'rs arrayed.
I taste unconscious every bliss of thine,
Thy weird enchantments and thy love divine;
And I could weep when morning glows again
To prove thy short-lived joys; but 'twould be vain,
For then I feel the breast once more supplied
With all those hopes with which the eve had died;
And living fires expand the system through,
With brighter aspects of life's distant view.
What though thy joys ephemeral may be,
From bondage but an hour to set me free?
All breathing nature finds in thee its rest,
All wounded hearts are by thee daily blest;
Wealthy or poor, on beds of down or straw,
It is the same, impartial is thy law.

F

But should we wish to look upon the past,
Or mourn felicity which could not last,
Or on our griefs reflect a little while,
Or hide the furrows with befitting smile,
Or share a project which we know not how,
And teach ourselves of some unwonted glow—
Then Sleep infusing, as our fancy gleams,
Spares us more fleeting joys—life-seeming dreams.

What is a dream?   Ought I physicians ask,
For know they not their own peculiar task?
Let them express opinions as they will,
I have my own, and these my fancy fill.
Dreams are like bubbles that a voyage take,
Pleasing with undulations that they make;
Slow turning round they show each Iris hue,
Now red or yellow, or cerulean blue:
Mounting aloft as if the clouds to meet,
On zephyrs borne, now circling, slow or fleet,
Further they sail, and when our hopes arise,
To see them pass from vision to the skies,
They burst asunder, yet we know not where,
Sudden they die and seem absorbed in air.
That once they shone we know, and nothing more;
No precious goods save vivid hues they bore;
Air but they were, to such they passed away,
And lived the stolen moments of a day:
Harmless and light, who ever such disdains?
They burst, and not a fragment then remains.
I love all dreams, for none can ever harm;
They soothe the bosom with an airy charm;
Fantastic or grotesque, and those that please
Our fondest expectations, never tease
My morning recollections when I wake,
Or hurt my feelings when the visions break.

Hope of my youth! I loved thee truly most,
To be some future day a public boast;
Eccentric shapes then danced before my sight,
And visionary gold enriched me quite.

There was a joy pugnacious in itself,
A forced reality in such wild pelf;
But youth's vagaries must be all forgiv'n,
Life is itself a hope to enter heav'n.
And when at night, unconscious in repose,
My pent-up thoughts were turned to dreamy shows,
My heart leapt forth, ecstatic to the core,
The throb was louder, smiles increased the more;
A hundred charms, a thousand blisses reigned,
And all their rosy welcomes I obtained:
My garb was altered, all I once did own,
My cottage roof to some palatial dome.
But, as experience tells us to this day,
The greater blessings sooner pass away,
Amid my wealth I would like Tantalus rise,
And gaze around with maniacal eyes:
The life unfeigned, the *real* state of things,
Was reckoned on imaginative wings;
But, ah! the dream though false, it played so well,
Its cheat without suspense I could not tell.

At first discouraged, soon I learned to bear
The forged enchantments from the world of care;
Joys could no more deceive, and as the dreams
Would come again with fresh and fairer themes,
In perfect measure would I sip their store,
And when I 'woke it was not to deplore.
Such had I found consistent with my views,
Bringing no melancholy to my Muse:
Bubbles I deemed them, histrionic play,
And without fail as such they passed away.

Dread of my riper days! prehensile woe,
That racks this short existence here below;
How does my heart complain of evil thee,
Combating with thyself for liberty?
Oh, sure I feel thee at this moment grind,
Polluting slow the empire of my mind;
But thou must sink, thy load thou canst not bear,
Whilst to my couch I trustingly repair;

I know thou canst not live, nor here remain,
Therefore I do not weep, I but complain.

At night's profoundest watch, serenest calm,
I welcome sleep to taste its mildest balm;
But through some evil watcher o'er the way,
Or by the dark forebodings of the day,
At times my rest is tortured by a dream
Of ugly notions, forms that real seem;
Indigence and grief approach on either side,
Misfortune gapes with sunken eyeballs wide;
Threatened by such I tremble to behold,
Enfeebling moisture from my brow runs cold;
With fright I gaze, I see some murd'rer nigh,
Vindictive is his wrath, and fire his eye;
He lifts his poniard—ah ! the awful steel—
He strikes, oh, where ?—My wak'ning doth reveal
The horrid cheat—how pleasing to survey,
The airy bubble, histrionic play?
And smiling at the dream with bosom light,
I feel unburdened while I bless the night.

Primeval days are but a dream at best,
For now alone our fancy they invest;
Ages thus fled to be no longer seen,
Have they not vanished like a morning dream ?
We gaze in wonder at their ancient glory,
Their deeds that live in everlasting story;
Their mammoth ruins, monster works of hand,
Still hold our admiration at command.
And though ungentle was their rule and pow'r,
And Science glimmered in her twilight hour,
Myriads of poets, sages, statesmen, rose,
And muscle won the battle between foes.
Moderns unnumbered still will scarce believe
The lurid past ; the dead cannot deceive:
Echoes e'en now we hear and footsteps faint,
Some walking spectre or mysterious saint ;
And all appears a dream since they have fled,
No more with us the living—but the dead.

Hush! let the Muse relate while fancy soars
The land of Hellas and its classic shores;
Or dips the wing within Parnassus' fount,
Or broods awhile to view the Pindus mount,
Where blithesome zephyrs through the year prevail,
And breathe the rapture of some sacred tale;
Striking their numbers o'er the pointed crags,
The grass-worn coverts and the water-flags;
The merry brooklets easy in their flow,
The sunlit slopings and the valleys low;
The distant echo of some happy bird,
Or sounds of woodland now in requiems heard;
The peaceful circuit of some guarded plain
By granite walls, or open to the main,
Where ceaseless breakers moan of ancient days,
Of trodden beauty, and departed rays
Of peerless splendour, and historic fame
That shook the nations, set the world aflame;
That hurled the foeman from its classic soil,
And prouder rose the greater its turmoil.

The gods revered have fled like other men,
Heard of alone, but never seen again;
Their mystic deeds are sung to happy lays,
Their wondrous pow'rs attuned to themes of praise,
Delphi the brave no longer calls to arms;
Pythia is dead, the virgin in her charms;
Apollo prompts no more what he would speak;
Lost is the tripod, though we fain would seek.
Athenè's pride has tumbled to the ground,
The sacred olives there no more abound;
The proud athlete bewails Olympia now,
The garland's faded that would crown his brow;
While Alpheus gently flows its course along,
With banks untrod, unknown to rapturous song.
The golden apples of Hesperides,
The lord of giants, mighty Hercules;
The Lernean hydra, and the royal beast,
The Minotaur and Bacchanalian feast;
Hector and Æneas; Achilles the brave,

To whom Vulcan the matchless armour gave;
Of Agamemnon, and the roving life
Of sage Ulysses and his virtuous wife;
The myriad sons of valour that arose
To save their land and extirpate its foes—
Who will relate? Have not the poets sung?
Have not their harps with sweetest numbers rung?
Sublimest notes they've struck, that never fail,
But echo music in each passing gale.
Homer and Hesiod, when their strains we hear,
Fast drops the unsophisticated tear;
The blood runs warm, the heart bounds forth with joy,
And distant visions round our being cloy:
Fancy still soaring high would have it seem
Though watchful, we are spell-bound in a dream.

Consider Rome and how her glories shone,
To dazzle those who gazed her empire on;
Her legions trampled o'er a thousand States,
Her eagles spread and held the Western Gates,
Where the Atlantic billows in its rage,
Or howls the anthem of a buried age.
Europa was her own: beneath her sway
She saw the nimbus of a brighter day;
The arts advanced and newer seeds were set,
Those that still flourish and instruct us yet:
The children rivalled, battled for renown,
While mother Rome to ruins tottered down.
No more is she the Rome of golden days,
What poets sing is not her living praise:
The twice two hundred nations Cæsar won
Have burst their shackles finding he is gone.
All this appears a dream; we know alone
That once there shone, and now but *stands*, a Rome.
And do we mourn that such was e'er her fate?
Nay, tyranny and pride did her inflate;
Her very sons she slew, the best she bore,
Rancid corruption worked within her core:
'Twas just that she should fall and pass away,
And be a moral to all future day.

All mortals have their dreams.   The tender child,
Whose forward hopes are fancifully wild,
Turns to his couch with blest assurance drawn,
Careless of pang or sorrow on the morn.
All-charming sleep then weighs his eyelids down,
There flies his brow Imagination's frown;
Inviting depths unfold their treasures vast,
He views and wishes they were all amassed:
Brief hesitation—and he rushes on;
The task commenced must not be left undone;
Fills to satiety and strives to gain
The cobweb ladder of all worldly fame.
On through the night his dreams are pleasing most;
Now calm at home, or on some foreign coast;
Now lord or master of some proud estate,
With much to love, and little e'er to hate:
Forsooth, his dreams, a half that they decree
But prove his madness in his vanity.
But as the morn comes laughing from the East,
To bid him stir, from lethean bonds released,
He runs and tells his mother every dream,
Solicits answer as to what they mean:
Dubious—not quite—he thinks they've prophesied
His future glory, his awaiting pride.
The smiling parent, happy in his joy,
Would not for worlds that balm of heart destroy;
Yet, fearing disappointment in the van
Might hurt the child ere it becomes a man,
Suspends a sigh and speaks in language terse—
" Dreams are not true ; just read them the reverse."
Disheartened for a time, to him 'tis strange
His dreams should altered be, the visions change ;
Till once again he plots and dreams at night
Of overtures that make him doubly blithe :
And thus occurring oft he thinks that they
Could never mean his senses to betray ;
Exulting then, on them he fain depends,
And tells the whole unto his schoolroom friends.

Fostered by Hope, expectantly sublime,
Years roll; he enters fearless on his prime;
School and its studies parted far behind,
A host of novel prospects seize his mind :
Lawyers and statesmen, merchants, hacks he sees,
Toilers and clerks of all the known degrees.
But life he finds is no consistent play ;
We gain by this and lose another way ;
Who can declare the much that we have lost ?
What we have won our very selves has cost.
His bark is launched on life's tumultuous sea,
Dangers surround and many rocks there be:
The faithful pilot *self* doth onward guide,
But deadly as the simoom is that pride
That breeds a hurricane in ev'ry blast,
And has the sky with thick'ning clouds o'ercast.
We must stoop down and let it pass us o'er,
Submissive be, nor speak nor murmur sore,
Until the whirl or vortex we have passed,
To reach a fragment of our hopes at last.
He who's in prime then learns the truth of dreams,
Vainglorious all, with but enchanting scenes,
And so forgives the follies of his youth,
'Twas then the flow'r and not the riper fruit.
And still he loves to picture joys again,
Though troubles work, disordering the brain;
He views in them no harm, however gay,
For theirs is but an innocent display,
That snatches grief from out the wearied breast,
Instilling balm, affording gentle rest.

List to a lover's dream at solemn night,
While Cynthia's lamp was coursing to its height,
While seraph stars blinked in th' etheral deep,
And chilly dews bespoke their want of sleep.
Pale was the glimmer of the lamp around,
No voice was heard, no cricket-throat did sound;
No gale without; the windows fast were closed,
And Philomel herself may have reposed:
Cosy in bed, no thought of earthly wiles,
He lay—the lover of a thousand smiles.

He dreamed a dream of most prolific sweets,
Such as the loving heart for e'er entreats;
A dream that speaks the advent of those joys
That knit together hours that love employs.
One he had loved for many a tedious day,
Whose woman-charms had robbed his heart away;
And begging for the treasure that sustained
His life, his being, gently he complained;
Spoke in disguise, his words were never plain,
And in this wise he merely sought in vain.
From tim'rous natures what can we expect?
Their hopes arise and are too swiftly wrecked:
A life's absorbing project, all its cost,
Might by a moment's fearing e'er be lost.
The lover dreamed he walked a gorgeous field,
Where trees their aromatic odours yield;
And looking to the East in solemn awe,
Beheld the lighter shades of evening draw:
And with them came the larks from dells and plains,
Dancing in air, attempting rural strains.
He onward paced and would have distant gone,
Where by hill-tops th' horizon was upborne,
Had not a maiden face to mem'ry known,
Lighted his eyes and raised the welcome tone:
" Ah, wherefore, Cyril, wouldst thou pass the eve?
Is there no heart that lists thee to believe?
Thine own Druscilla patiently awaits
To clasp thy form within her garden gates."
" Say, does she love?" " She loves thy very self;
And gives no thought to others nor to pelf;
Gentle and kind, her heart can fondness speak;
But woman, Cyril, thou must know, is weak.
Go plead from her the heart that thou wouldst share,
And lay thine own within her bosom fair:
Do not alone within her sunshine bask;
How canst thou get when thou wilt never ask?"
" 'Tis true; but in my breast there lived a fear
I'd be denied the heart so truly dear;
And if thou knowest I could it obtain,
Then I will ask and may not seek in vain."

" She's told me oft her heart's for thee alone ;
Go be a man and pledge with her thine own."

The dream departed, and those eyes awoke
To sleep no more that night.   When morn had broke
He courage took, bade fainting thought adieu,
And wished to learn if what he dreamt was true.
Seeking the face to him the most divine,
He knelt and pleaded at her queenly shrine ;
Received a thousand smiles, the fond caress,
Which sighs and troubles all within suppress :
United hearts no more to be dismayed—
Who can pronounce the dream had falsely played ?

Our dreams are often true.   In them there lies
A future unperceived by mortal eyes ;
A stern reality, a joy or sorrow,
That comes apace and breaks seal with the morrow.
Empiric oft bethought, we learn that dreams
Not always are facetious, airy schemes ;
They come as warnings from yon starry dome,
To have us fit prepared for what may come ;
For joy or sorrow unexpected may
Deaden the pulse and rob the soul away.
'Tis oft the case.   Once had I known a youth
Firm in his faith and taught to love the truth ;
Who kept his own opinions to himself,
And troubled not with those who strove for pelf ;
Who toiled for honour's sake and honest gain,
Whom failure fired and victory made not vain.
His means were mediocre, and he lived
At envied ease, as if of nought deprived ;
When bounding to his feet one day was told
Of one who died and left him all his gold.
The wealth was great, too great for sudden joy,
Dazzling the eyes of that unthinking boy :
He ranted, revelled, rotted to the core,
Drowsied by drink he only cried for more ;
Disease approached, pangs tortured ev'ry side,
And in a madness without pray'r he died.

Poets have had their dreams, and such they wrote;
Their sacred visions round our being float;
Their faithful colours move within the air,
Like those of Iris, fresh, divine, and fair.
Delight and wonder, thoughts that cling to please,
Possess the man who Shakespeare's volume sees:
Villains and saints, oh, what a motley crew,
Described therein, all perfect life and true.
Monarchs and statesmen, parasites demure,
Wits who destroy the spleen by laughter's cure;
Fairies and witches, demons that have fled,
Battles victorious, of the mighty dead;
Heroes and men from out the darkest mist,
Charactered in full, as even *now* exist;
Princes and peasants, all we see and find,
The various specimens of womankind;
The thousand woes that eat the flesh explained,
The incubus that would our blood have drained;
The blisses that instil the purest balm,
The day's wild tempest and nocturnal calm—
These we behold therein: ah! where's the world?
Its darkest mysteries are there unfurled;
Its laws, its natures, all examined keen:
Oh, what an Atlas Shakespeare must have been!

In thought ecstatic and in words sublime,
Milton comes forth to tune the graceful Nine;
The holy flashes play about his eye,
He strikes his numbers and the Gorgons sigh.
Heaven beholds her Muse-inspired son,
Aids in the glorious task he has begun;
The clouds roll past, the very air is still,
While Phœbus leans upon some neighb'ring hill.
The minstrel sings, what sparks escape the lyre!
His words are solace and yet made of fire:
He mourns corruption within ev'ry state,
Man's disobedience and accursed fate;
Renounces hell while Satan hides his face
And dares not list the tale of his disgrace.

On runs the theme, unfolding joys are there;
A master sings with superhuman care;
A bosom throbs where no deception reigns,
A tongue relates of Heav'n's unseen domains.
The past has fled: Emmanuel parts the gloom,
Destroys the shackles that would seal our doom;
Throws wide the doors of His celestial home,
And welcomes one and all who meekly come.
Thus sings the minstrel with stentorian voice,
Bidding the nations rise up and rejoice;
And as he sings an epic floats along,
The grandest theme devoted e'er to song.

Where Otway pictured and where Jonson slept,
The fairies loiter and the Muse has wept;
Unnumbered tears, like dews of early morn,
Steep down the graves of poets once forlorn.
The Thespian world their absence mourns in vain,
They've fled no more to view these scenes again;
The wood-nymphs linger discontented quite;
A requiem breathes, yet no returning sprite:
There, at those tombs, unyielding in their trust.
The gods surround to watch the sacred dust.
Swift with imagination cleaves the blast,
Beyond the cold North star his eye has passed;
Lands he surveys and wondrous realms anew,
Where ne'er the faithful needle pointed to.
In classic diction Addison prevails,
The gifted magus of a thousand tales;
Learn of his prose teeming with thought sublime,
Drink deep the nectar of platonic rhyme:
He lights a newer era to his praise,
And lesser lamps convert it to a blaze.

Oh, generous Goldsmith, by thy sylvan flute
Age has been charmed with terpsichorean youth;
But when the lyre was snatched from its repose,
And when thy fingers—as thy breast arose—
Trembled upon its strings, was Nature pleased,
Unworthy brawls and tumults were appeased;

The sense of lovely thought would fill the brain,
And as thou'dst cease we'd wish to hear again.
Ungrateful world that saw thee from a child
Plodding through life, lost in its mazes wild;
Inhuman hearts that had thee borne away
'Neath Gallic skies to bright Italian day';
A wand'ring exile from thy native shore,
From where a *chain** was tethered to thy core:
Rash as they were, they drank thy blisses up,
And left thee nothing but the empty cup.

Why speak of Savage? "Hush!" the winds exclaim;
" England is silent, conscious of her shame:
She crowns with laurels fresh the minstrel's brow,
And only wishes he were living now:
Proud of her son, his merits she has found,
And breathes his music to the world around."
England repentant! No, that cannot be;
Oh, soothe my breast and dash the tear from me.
Sad fearings now into my visions creep,
And voices call as from the midnight deep.
I see a spectral Otway move along;
A murmur dies, the fragment of a song;
Deep marks are on his face; 'tis ghastly pale;
His last footstep has echoed in the gale.
I see another through a parting cloud:
'Tis Chatterton, he trails a long-worn shroud:
How youthful does he seem! his cheek is damp;
But on his brow is Meditation's stamp:
One look he casts, one sigh vibrates the air,
And he has fled from out this world of care.

All poet's dreams are lovely, with their views,
Their strains of melody and varied hues;
True in the cadences that rouse the heart,
They paint with love and happy views impart;
Lighting on all with wands of fairy elves,
They're fretful only when they paint themselves.

* Still to my brother turns with ceaseless pain,
And drags at each remove a length'ning chain.—Goldsmith's *Traveller.*

Borne in the bounding tenant of the brine,
The fearless sailor views some distant clime;
Or sees the billows swell around his form,
As if to tell of some approaching storm.
He casts his longing eyes above the mast,
The tiny pennant shivers in the blast;
But ev'ry cloud is still, no petrel flies,
Apollo smiles within his native skies.
Below, the hissing foam is white as fleece,
Playing in circles, now on the increase,
Then parting far, or rising with the spray,
Or o'er the liquid hills to roll away.
No land from yonder dim horizon peeps,
No distant bark like some lorn phantom sweeps;
A waste of waters and a world of fears,
Groanings that fall around hoar Neptune's ears.
He—the mariner of a thousand storms—
Whiffs at his pipe, or the fierce tumult scorns;
Sits at the fore with gusto to his prog,
Or slowly walks astern to heave the log.
Watchful at night, he guards a flying hour,
Stands at the bow while denser shadows lower;
Views a strange light and counts the stars in vain,
Runs o'er the Milky Way, or neighbouring main,
Where phosphorescent flashes play at will,
In various shapes—and him with wonder fill.
A rude philosophy does questions raise
Till he rejects the problem in a maze;
And when the watch is o'er, he strikes the bell,
Shouts to the pacing mate a hoarse " All's well!"

Snug in his berth, he thinks once more of home,
Recalls to mind the heart he's left alone,
And in his silence feels that he could weep,
Throw off his hat and sail no more the deep.
Tender as any child, his bosom heaves,
To recollections fond his fancy cleaves;
He hears a comrade snore, a foot on deck,
But turns to sleep, fearless of storm or wreck.
Then visions crowd; he dreams of bygone days,
When by his native beach he sang his lays;

Sat on the rocks to view the sun go down,
Or count the vessels as they passed the town ;
Thinks of his earlier age ; the corks he threw,
The bits of timber, on the wavelet blue ;
The first sweet face that bade his bosom move,
The first soft ear in which he whispered love.

Oh, airy blisses ! Oh, beguiling pow'rs !
Morpheus, I thank thee for thy pleasing hours ;
But let me cease, thou wilt not hear of praise :
The sailor dreams again—of riper days.
Now, in his Nancy's arms he breathes a pray'r
That Providence might bless his darling fair ;
And as she tells of all her fearings sore,
He promises to never leave her more ;
Draws forth his kerchief, wipes her streaming eyes,—
" Cheer up, my birdie "—here the dream it flies.
He lights his pipe and deems it ne'er the worse,
The more he roams more full will be his purse ;
And thanks the dream that taught him how to trace
So well the beauties of his Nancy's face ;
That let him pass a moment by her side,
Though in his waking far he was and wide :
He hopes the sweet deceit will come again,
And asks himself if e'er she dreams the same.

Upon the field the soldier moves along,
In rank and file o'er fifty thousand strong ;
On ev'ry side the breast is beating loud,
And every face is timorously proud ;
Whilst fast the foes like wolves come tearing down,
Thirsting for blood, for honour and renown,
With flags and standards floating in the wind,
And polished steel that glitters most unkind.
He thinks of home, the cherished ones behind,
And that one thought's corroding in his mind ;
A pang, an anguish lingers in his heart,
As if the last life-drops would soon depart.
A word, a call ; the signal gun is giv'n,
The shout goes up, the smoky air is riv'n ;

Sulphurous vapours cloud the awful scene,
Dishevelled rays from heaven intervene;
Inflated pride and vengeance mark each face;
Who will survive the honour or disgrace?
The bloody torrent pours with greater tide,
Destruction works, death is on ev'ry side;
Unsheathéd sabres wash themselves in gore,
Mad'ning the cannonade's continuous roar;
The crowded missiles wildly twain the blast;
How many mortals there behold their last!

Eve in her dusky brown now ventures nigh;
But hark, yon bugle! doleful is its cry:
Behold the foe retreating o'er the way;
They turn, they fly, and leave to us the day:
Demoralised, hard pressed are they for breath,
And half their number pallid lie in death.

The hapless soldier moaning o'er his wounds,
Half shuts his eyes in torture, and half swoons;
With agony he breathes; his breast is cold,
The fire extinguished that once made it bold;
Upon his lips a gentle quiv'ring plays;
Oh, for a draught how great would be his praise!
Life, he believes, would warm as e'er before;
Give him a few cold drops—he asks no more.

Forth from the ashen clouds the moon appears,
Pale as a frighted maid, with dewy tears,
Stoops o'er the stricken forms and stares aghast
At Pride demeaned, Ambition damped at last.
From out her lamp the silv'ry beams divide,
Casting a glimmer o'er the country wide;
While all around seems wrapt in wicked trance,
Till midnight ghouls in airy forms advance.

The landscape rears; the mounds and plains reveal
The ghastly horrors of the awful scene,
The scattered glories of the sov'reign Mars,
The subtle engines of but barb'rous wars.

The soldier turns ; he sees his comrades pale ;
He hears their dreadful groans or dying tale ;
Shudders at ev'ry thought with gaze intent,
Awaits the turn of his predicament.
Athwart he views the forms of living men,
That stoop and rise, and stoop low down again ;
Like shadows they beseem, spectres at best,
That rob or give the dead and dying rest.
Slumber steals o'er his brow, and on that spot
His own fierce agony is soon forgot ;
In life's full energy he bounds the while ;
His wife is in his arms, his children smile ;
The house dog barks and strives to gain his knee,
Sunshine and peace present their every glee,
His sword is sheathed and no wild trumpets call,
His empty gun hangs idly on the wall:—
These work deception to a real seeming,
And constitute the pleasures of his dreaming.

These are the joys oblivious hours supply,
That dreams can offer when we gently lie,
To seek that solace which the world denies,
In active life beneath the noonday skies;
To breathe in slumber, heedless of the dawn,
And marry life unto another morn:
To teach and cultivate and plainly show
Nothing is certain on this world below,
Aye, not an atom: all is fated sure;
Nothing beneath yon azure dome is pure.
And, what is life?   Hearken: it is a dream,
Picturing things that are not what they seem ;
Far it allures, and bursts at death, when we—
Behold ourselves in yon eternity !

MELBOURNE:

M'CARRON, BIRD AND CO., PRINTERS,

479 COLLINS ST.

www.ingramcontent.com/pod-product-compliance
Lightning Source LLC
Chambersburg PA
CBHW021420090426
42742CB00009B/1198